> *"This time, like all times, is a very good one if we know what to do with it."*
>
> —Ralph Waldo Emerson

How to Make
Every Day
Independence Day

How to Make Every Day Independence Day
Dr. Steve W. Price

Copyright 2012 by Steve W. Price
Published by Metaphor Press

Metaphor Press
10427 Orange Grove Dr.
Tampa, FL 33618

Distributed exclusively through:
Kat Ranch Marketing
P.O. Box 396
Morehead City, NC 28557

ISBN: 978-0-9822549-3-6
Published by Metaphor Press

Printed in United States of America

Cover design and text layout by Parry Design Studio, Inc.

OTHER BOOKS BY DR. STEVE W. PRICE

Household Gold

How to Bounce When Others Break

Dream Making in a Dream-Taking World

WWW. Stands for "World Wide Whiners"

Surviving the Perfect Recession

DEDICATION

To Mary and Ernie Price, my mom and dad, for backing my decision in 1986 to resign from a "secure job" to pursue my dream of owning my own life by owning my own business.

Most of all, thank you for your unconditional love. I've doubted myself from time to time, but I've never doubted your love. Not for a moment. Thank you for being... you.

CONTENTS

Independence Is an Inborn Drive

INTRODUCTION

Independence Is an Inborn Drive

It is by freedom that a man knows himself, by his sovereignty over his own life that a man measures himself.

—Elie Wiesel
from "What Really Makes Us Free?"

O f all the holidays in all the countries around the globe, Independence Day is by far the most common and most celebrated.

As I write this, 152 of the world's 194 countries celebrate Independence Day or its equivalent, National Day—overwhelming proof that the desire for freedom resides deep within the human heart, resonating across continents... across countries... and across cultures.

From the world's first Declaration of Independence in A.D. 301, when the tiny European nation of San Marino declared its independence from the Roman Empire (and amazingly, 1,700 years later, still remains a separate, sovereign nation), human history has been on a long, steady march toward freedom and away from political domination by kings, tyrants, and dictators.

1

Independence Is in Our DNA

"The history of the world is none other than the progress of the consciousness of freedom," wrote the 19th century German philosopher George Hegel. His observation rings truer today than ever before, as the battle for independence continues to rage in more than a dozen countries around the globe.

In the Middle East and North Africa, for example, "Arab Spring" has inspired millions of oppressed citizens in freedom-starved countries to flood the streets demanding basic freedoms and democratic elections. It's too early to tell if the overthrow of tyrannical governments across the Arab world will end with truly democratic governments or if the rebellions will wind up exchanging one form of oppressive government for another; but the intent of the protestors and armed rebels is clear—the inner drive for freedom is so deeply imbedded in the DNA of humans that, across time and cultures, people are willing to sacrifice their lives for independence.

Two Types of Tyrannies

"The tyrannies are doomed," says Bernard Lewis, a leading scholar of the Arab world. Thanks to free-flowing information via the Internet and constant connectivity via smartphones in the hands of the masses, Lewis is correct as far as governments are concerned—the days of state-controlled governments are drawing to a close.

But as I see it, there are two types of tyranny, and they both seek to limit our independence. The first type, **external tyranny**, is a *top-down tyranny* imposed by a few power-drunk dictators. North Korea is a prime example of external tyranny, whereby the all-powerful state controls the populace by limiting personal independence of its citizens. Although weakened in recent years, external tyranny still restricts the freedoms of nearly half of the 7 billion people around the globe.

The second type of tyranny, **internal tyranny**, is a *bottom-up tyranny* imposed, ironically, on the masses by themselves. Internal tyranny is characterized by negative self-talk and faulty personal belief systems that lead to bad habits... action-freezing fears... faulty conclusions...

rationalizations… justifications… and insecurities, causing people to act voluntarily in ways that limit their God-given right to independence.

Internal tyranny causes people to give themselves mental marching orders that keep them dependent on dead-end jobs… in debt… underachieving… overweight… and out of shape, just to name a few common self-imposed restrictions on independence.

That's why I say that if you live in a democracy, the greatest threat to your independence is yourself.

A Classic Example of Internal Tyranny

If you are a fan of the Food Channel, you've likely seen Paula Deen, the queen of ultra-unhealthy, deep-fat-fried, butter- and calorie-laden dishes that sound more like a skit on *Saturday Night Live* than for-real recipes. Here are a few of the recipes that helped her transition from housewife to household name: deep-fried Twinkies… fried butter balls… deep-fried chocolate-covered cheese cake… and her signature artery-clogging sandwich, a double bacon cheeseburger and fried egg between two glazed donuts. I wish I were making this up—I'm not.

In defense of her unhealthy recipes, Deen quips, "I'm your cook, not your doctor." Well, now the 65-year-old Deen is the one who needs a doctor, having been diagnosed in 2009 with type 2 diabetes, a healthcare crisis all by itself, affecting almost 10% of the U.S. population and costing $175 billion annually. Type 2 diabetes is the seventh-leading cause of death in the U.S. and a major contributor to heart disease, kidney failure, blindness, amputations, and strokes.

For sure, Deen's name-branded products—from TV shows and cookbooks to eyeglasses and furniture—have made her *financially independent*.

But the price she has to pay is *dependence on diabetes drugs* (which she has parlayed into a money-making role as spokeswoman for the drug company Novo Nordisk, which makes and markets diabetes drugs).

Deen's **internal tyrant** dictated that she promote recipes that please the palate but poison the body, not only a poor lifestyle choice for herself

3

and her family, but also endangering the health of millions of admirers who gulp down her recipes. Celebrity chef Anthony Bourdain is bold in his criticism of Deen's unhealthy recipes, calling her, "the worst, most dangerous person in America" and scolding her for making money by advertising drugs that treat a largely preventable disease, type 2 diabetes, that her recipes contribute to.

In a free society, Deen can promote whatever foods she chooses—I'm all in favor of that. But people who cook her way and eat her way for long are going to have health issues, and Paula Deen, whether she admits it or not, must take some responsibility for contributing to obesity, the number one risk factor for developing diabetes later in life.

Retraining Your Internal Tyrant

Unlike **external tyrants**, who must be removed by force, *internal tyrants* (that is, the mental messages we tell ourselves) can be retrained. That's the beauty of free will—we're free to rethink our old thoughts and, as a result, manifest new behaviors: overweight people can start eating healthier... out of shape people can start exercising... people living paycheck to paycheck can start saving... dependent people can start expressing their independence.

The first step is to think new, positive, can-do thoughts.

The second step is to act on those thoughts.

For an example of someone who changed their life by changing their thinking, I return, surprisingly, to Paula Deen. In 1986, Deen moved from her hometown of Albany, Georgia, to Savannah when her husband changed jobs. She thought it was the worst thing that ever happened. "I thought my life was over," she later recalled. "I spent two months in bed, crying."

Her depression deepened into *agoraphobia*, the psychological term for fear of open spaces, and Deen didn't leave her house for five years. Then one day she got out of bed and the Serenity Prayer came into her head:

"That particular morning I understood what it was saying," she told a reporter for *Newsweek* magazine. "I understood what I was supposed to be asking God for—it was the wisdom to accept the things I couldn't

4

change and the courage to change the things I could. I got up and I said, 'I've got to make some changes. For one, I had to start standing on my own feet.'"

With only $200 as seed money, she started a business called The Bag Lady, making bag lunches and sending her children to sell them to workers in the neighborhood. A year and a half later, she opened her own restaurant—and things snowballed from there.

"My advice to people," Deen says, "would be to keep your head high and your eyes open, 'cause you never know what God has got in store for you. You can't limit yourself or your possibilities."

When Life Becomes a Battleground, Your Mind Is Your Best Weapon

I admire Deen's decision to face her fears and embrace new possibilities by venturing out of her house and opening a restaurant, a courageous act that began a basket of blessings beyond her wildest dreams. By taking control of her mental dictator and changing "I can't" thoughts to "I can" thoughts, she opened the door to independence and continues to reap the benefits 25 years later.

But the battle to control our interior tyrant *and remain independent in all areas of our lives* is never ending, and as much as Deen deserves our praise for becoming *financially independent*, she also deserves our criticism for advocating meals that made her (and perhaps thousands of her loyal followers) *physically dependent* on type 2 diabetes drugs.

Look, the purpose of this book isn't to chastise Paula Deen for becoming successful by serving up unhealthy food, anymore than I would chastise McDonald's for doing the same. No one is forcing people to supersize their fries or whip up Deen's recipe for her 12,000-calorie Krispy Kreme bread pudding.

But Deen is a great example of how free will can be used to *hurt ourselves...* as well as *help ourselves.*

Yes, independence opens doors to endless positive possibilities, but it also allows us to make unhealthy choices that circle back to dependence on drugs... or debt... or unemployment checks... or, as is the case with millions of aging Americans, a monthly Social Security check as the sole means of support during retirement.

Honor Your God-Given Gifts

I'll close with a story about another famous American, the legendary singer Tony Bennett. During the anything-goes-1970s, fame and money went to Bennett's head, and he began messing with cocaine. A chance conversation with a top Hollywood talent manager changed all that.

"The manager told me he used to handle a famous comic who became a heroin addict, later dying from an overdose," Bennett said. "I told him I knew the guy, and I asked the manager what he thought of him. The manager said one sentence that changed my life: 'He sinned against his talent.' And when I heard that sentence, I realized that's what I was doing. And I stopped everything that day."

He sinned against his talent—what a great line, and what an apt description of people who self-destruct from overindulging bad habits.

To a degree, we're all guilty of sinning against our talents, aren't we?

When I procrastinate working on a new book, for example, I'm sinning against my talent.

When Paula Deen chose to promote high-calorie, life-shortening recipes, she sinned against her talent. (Her youngest son, Bobby, has repented, so to speak. He now has a show on the Food Network called, *Not My Mamma's Meals*, in which he remakes her most heart-stopping dishes by substituting healthier ingredients.)

What about you? Are you guilty of sinning against your talents?

If you're staying in a dead-end job just for the paycheck...

If you're eating too much and exercising too little...

If you're using credit cards to finance a lifestyle you can't afford...

If you're spending more time with friends than you are with family...

If you're texting more than actually talking...

If you're spending more time planning your vacations than planning your retirement...

If you're still dreaming of owning your own business but aren't doing anything to make it happen...

... then you're sinning against your talents.

To live, and love, a life of independence, you must embrace and honor your talents instead of ignoring or neglecting them.

How This Book Can help

The purpose of this book is to give you the information and, hopefully, the inspiration that will help you to express independence in the key areas of your life—financial independence... emotional independence... physical independence... career independence... and eventually, retirement independence.

"We used tools in the past to leverage our muscles," Bill Gates said. "We use tools today to leverage our minds."

Think of this book as a tool to leverage your mind... to pry open your mind to the possibilities of enjoying more independence in your life... to persuade you to resist the Big Lie that dependence on a job or the government or a pill will make you happier than independence... and finally, to suggest strategies that can help you make every day Independence Day.

Unlike dependence, which smothers pride with the false promise of security, independence requires will power. And effort. And yes, courage. But the results are worth the effort.

Recommit Yourself to Independence

Need more proof that independence is an inborn drive? Of the 152 (and counting) free countries in the world, how many have voluntarily reinstated a conquering country or restored an ousted dictator because the citizens preferred the security of dependence more than the responsibility of independence?

The answer: Zero.

I wrote this book to encourage you to recommit yourself to your inborn drive for independence that impels us humans to step out of the soul-suffocating fog of dependence... to seek the sunlight of self-reliance... and, in doing so, to reach our highest potential.

Ben Franklin summed up the prominent position of independence to every freedom-loving person: *"People who give up essential liberty to obtain a little temporary safety deserve neither liberty nor safety."*

If you, like Ben Franklin and me and millions of others, prefer essential liberty to temporary safety, then turn the page to begin learning how to live, and love, a life of independence.

Don't Fall for the Big Lie

Don't Fall for the Big Lie

The more we have dependence on the government, the more people relying on entitlements become an interest group voting to maintain those entitlements.

—Gary Becker,
free-market economist

For thousands of years, humans have fought and died for independence... for the self-evident right to control their own destiny.

Then, in the mid-20th century, within just two generations, the many-thousand-year-old march toward freedom in democracies around the globe ground to a stop.

One by one, the marchers turned and moved, zombie-like, in the opposite direction, *away from individual freedom and toward dependence* on state-sponsored "social security" programs, laying down the welcome mat to the growing, freedom-gobbling Welfare State.

Buying the Big Lie

Let's get real here. All governments—dictatorships and democracies alike—are in the *dependency business*. That's how politicians stay in

11

power and collect their paychecks. Different systems of government just require that politicians use different means to justify their ends.

Dictatorships use violence to keep their people dependent.

Democracies use votes to keep their people dependent.

Dictators use a heavy hand to keep their people dependent—and it works until the people rebel.

Democracies use sleight-of-hand to keep their people dependent—and it works until the country goes broke, which is what is happening to scores of Western democracies, with five or 10 European nations leading the way and the U.S. following closely behind.

What happened? What went wrong? What caused some of the most independent, most prosperous countries in the history of the world to blow through trillions of dollars like a drunk teenager with Warren Buffet's credit card?

The answer is sadly simple—people in democracies fell for the Big Lie.

Politicians sold the Big Lie. And voters bought the Big Lie.

The Big Lie goes like this:

Vote for me and I'll give you cradle-to-grave job security... a government-funded early retirement... "free" healthcare... and generous unemployment benefits. Oh, best of all, it won't cost you anything. It's a free lunch, compliments of your warm and cuddly Big Government.

The Big Government Giveaway

The vast majority of thinking people would agree that there's nothing wrong with government programs that provide a *temporary* safety net to give citizens a hand up in tough times. But the problem is that over time, "temporary" social safety nets turn into permanent hammocks for the unmotivated people who become dependent on handouts.

A case in point: In 1970, *3 million* Americans were receiving food stamps at a cost of $270 million a year. Four decades later, a record *40 million people* were enrolled in the program, costing taxpayers $58

12

billion in 2010, a nearly 20-fold increase in dependence on the federal government.

"We need less entitlement growth and more personal growth," I wrote in 2009 in my best-selling book, *Surviving the Perfect Recession*. "We need to warn people away from entitlements—they dull ambition, reward sloth, discourage risk-taking, and destroy dreams."

Oh, and if that's not enough, entitlements turn once-prosperous nations into deep-debtor nations, which is occurring in countries across Europe and has turned the United States, the world's biggest economy, into the world's biggest debtor in only five decades.

How did we get in this mess? How could a dozen of the world's biggest economies turn prosperity into penury in only 50 years following the end of WWII? Answer: By telling voters the Big Lie—promising voters government giveaways so generous that no nation could afford them.

The Story of the Shopping Wife

The Big Lie reminds me of a story:

Several men are sitting at a table in the locker room of a golf club. A cellphone rings and a man engages the hands-free speaker function and begins to talk. Everyone else in the room stops to listen.

MAN: "Hello?"

WOMAN: "Hi Honey, it's me. Are you at the club?"

MAN: "Yes."

WOMAN: "I'm at the shops now and found this beautiful leather coat. It's only $2,000. Is it OK if I buy it?"

MAN: "Sure, go ahead if you like it that much."

WOMAN: "I also stopped by the Lexus dealership and saw the new models. I saw one I really liked."

MAN: "How much?"

WOMAN: "$90,000."

MAN: "OK, but for that price I want it with all the options."

WOMAN: "Great! Oh, and one more thing. I was just talking to Janie and found out that the house I wanted last year is back on the market. They're asking $980,000 for it."

MAN: "Well, then go ahead and make an offer of $900,000. They'll probably take it. If not, we can go the extra $80,000 if it's what you really want."

WOMAN: "OK. I'll see you later! I love you so much!"

MAN: "Bye! I love you, too."

The man hangs up. The other men in the locker room are staring at him in astonishment, mouths wide open.

He turns and asks, "Anyone know whose phone this is?"

Great story, huh? And it's an apt fable for modern-day welfare states that promise more than they can deliver. Think of the man in the story as a politician seeking reelection. The woman is a voter seeking a free lunch. For the woman, it's easy to ask for the moon. For the man, it's easy (and fun) to give (after all, it's not HIS money). But what about the *real* husband in the story—the taxpayer—the one footing the bill for this spending spree? What happens when he finds out about the consequences of his wife buying into the Big Lie? He'll be the one holding the bag when the bill comes due… and he's going to be angry—VERY angry—and in debt up to his eyeballs.

Dependence on the Government Increasing

Nearly 50 years ago, Lain Macleod, a conservative member of the English Parliament, coined the term "Nanny State" to describe government's overly generous and overly protective welfare programs designed by liberal politicians to insulate citizens "against the risks and hazards of life," to use Franklin Roosevelt's words.

Ironically, citizens of countries that fought valiantly for freedom and independence during WWII started relinquishing their personal freedoms in exchange for social security from the government, blatantly ignoring

Thomas Jefferson's sage appeal for small government: *"The government is best which governs least because its people discipline themselves."*

Casting self-reliance to the wind, citizens in Western democracies voted for politicians who promised to expand "free" government programs. The result: The welfare state's unrestrained growth will seduce millions of citizens into dependency on government services. Here are a few Nanny State excesses that threaten to usurp our freedoms and bankrupt countries:

In the United States:

- 44% of the U.S. population is living in a household receiving some kind of government benefits, more than any time in history.

- 60% of the federal budget is spent on entitlement programs, mostly Social Security and Medicare, at a time when 10,000 citizens a day turn 65 years old with an average life expectancy of 82.

- 47 of the 50 states have budget shortfalls for fiscal year 2011 while over-generous public pensions are underfunded by trillions.

In the United Kingdom:

- Almost 4 million of Britain's 20 million households have no one who earns a wage.

- 33% of the households rely on state handouts for more than half their annual income.

- 20% of the country's labor force has government jobs.

In Continental Europe:

- *In France,* 1 million protesters shut down Paris to rail against the government's proposal to raise the retirement age from 60 to 62.

- *In Greece,* the government employs 25% of the working population... pays them three times more money than private sector workers... and mandates retirement with full pay at age 50. The result—the government owes $250,000 for every working Greek.

- *In Denmark,* laid-off Danes who have worked 52 weeks over the previous three years are eligible to receive 90% of their average earnings for up to four years.

These budget-busting government benefits in the U.S. and Europe are just a sampling of the many generosities of Nanny States and how they reward slothful citizens while penalizing the most productive. But there is a double-edged downside to generous entitlements: scores of Nanny States in the West find themselves teetering on the brink of bankruptcy from decades of overspending on entitlement programs, while their benefit-addicted citizens riot over proposed reforms to reduce huge deficits by cutting entitlements.

As the news programs will confirm almost daily in the coming years, entitlements are *easy to give away...* but *tough to take away.* Expect to see on your TV and laptop a lot more battle lines... broken windows... and tears.

Recommitting Ourselves to Independence

I'm not saying that you're part of the problem—as you can see from the above statistics, the majority of citizens are *makers,* working and paying their taxes, to support a minority of *takers.* Unfortunately, *the takers have been growing in numbers,* year after year after year, with no end in sight.

The problem is that for decades now, the governments of industrialized nations, especially those in the West, have been systematically creating a *culture of dependence* through expanded state-sponsored social programs. And that insidious culture of dependence is a creeping threat to *your* independence.

Seventy-five years ago, a powerful politician described the danger of government dependence spreading from the makers to the takers... leaping from the truly needy to the simply greedy. His words are more relevant today than they were when he first spoke them 75 years ago:

> The lessons of history... show conclusively that continued dependence upon relief induces a spiritual and moral disintegration fundamentally destructive to the national fiber. To dole out relief in this way is to administer a narcotic, a subtle destroyer of the human spirit.

Ironically, the speaker was President Franklin D. Roosevelt, the architect of the American Nanny State, at his 1935 State of the Union address. FDR was fearful that his welfare programs might lure normally self-reliant people to start depending on the government to support their lifestyle. He was right to be concerned, for his warning became a reality for tens of millions of able-bodied people addicted to government handouts.

FDR may have ushered in our growing addiction to entitlements. And for the nearly 70 years since his death, politicians in both parties have added to the entitlement larder.

But now it's up to each of us, starting with you and me, to end our dependence on the government by replacing the Big Lie with the Big Truth—democracies have made promises they cannot keep, and the only way out of this mess is for people to live, and love, a life of independence.

Dependence Leads to Delusion

Dependence
Leads to Delusion

*Pennies do not come from heaven. They have to be
earned here, on Earth.*

—Margaret Thatcher,
on government giveaways

Some years ago, a mock political party in Latin America made a
spoof of campaign promises by pledging to save motorists money on gas
by building highways that only ran downhill.

They got lots of votes. Which is scarier than it is funny.

The unrealistic promises that politicians in industrialized countries
have made to voters are nearly as comical and far-fetched, not to mention
unaffordable. The only thing sadder than politicians making promises
that taxpayers can't keep is that millions of voters believe those promises.

Yep, and all the highways will run downhill....

That's why I say *dependence leads to delusion*. Some people actually
believe the pie-in-the-sky promises of politicians... actually believe that
the Nanny State will take care of all their wants and needs... actually
believe that Social Security and Medicare and state pensions and municipal
pensions don't need fixing and will never run out of money.

21

Yep, and all the highways will run downhill....

Voters hitching free rides on the government giveaway bus are so deluded they actually believe 1% of the wealthiest taxpayers can support 40% of the people who pay zero federal income tax. And then one day, the Nanny State bus will find itself stuck at the bottom of a long, steep highway with no gas in the tank. On that day, the politicians driving the bus will have to ask voters to get out and push.

For many democracies, that day has already arrived.

Light Pollution Resembles Political Pollution

How did so many people get so delusional as to think they are *entitled* to cradle-to-grave giveaways paid for by others and that governments can pull money out of thin air like a magician pulling bunnies out of a top hat?

I have the answer—I call it the "Firefly Theory."

Here's how it works: When I was a kid, part of summer fun was chasing fireflies on warm evenings. When night descended, dozens of fireflies floated across front lawns, and our neighborhood sparkled like a blinking galaxy as we chased the tiny blinking lights until our parents called us in for baths and bedtime.

Unfortunately, say scientists, our children may not enjoy those same memories because fireflies are disappearing. Why? *Light pollution.* Researchers theorize that artificial light from expanding development is a big contributor to dwindling firefly populations. You see, fireflies use their flashing lights to communicate—to attract mates and mark their territory. But as development spreads, lights from highways, homes, cars, stores, and streetlights compete with firefly flash patterns. All this bright artificial light is interfering with fireflies' communication systems and disorienting them to the point they can't distinguish real fireflies from passing car headlights. The result is a drastic drop in firefly populations.

Now, here's how the firefly theory applies to people:

Just as *light pollution* is disorienting fireflies by messing up their inborn navigation systems, *political pollution* (the political equivalent of artificial light) is messing up our mental and moral compasses. Voters are blinded by the bright-light promises of too-generous public pensions... disoriented by entitlements that, like a modern-day Robin Hood, take from the "greedy" rich and give to the "exploited" poor... and deceived by unsustainable senior-security programs that provide financial support and low-cost healthcare services to a growing number of elderly.

Political pollution corrupts our ability to be logical... to perform simple arithmetic... and to anticipate unintended consequences. As a result, our dependence on government leads to delusion, which leads to more dependence, which leads to more delusion.

And the beat goes on and on and on and on....

Disappearance of Pride

Do you remember the scene in the movie *Cinderella Man* where James J. Braddock, the heavyweight boxing champion during the Great Depression, stood in line at the public assistance office to *return* the money he received while on welfare. That scene actually happened in real life. Braddock considered the relief money he took as a loan to be repaid, not a wage to be kept. When the story broke in the newspapers prior to his epic fight with Max Baer, Braddock became an even bigger hero to the throngs of people down on their luck during the worst economic period in American history.

You see, Braddock's moral compass was working like it should have, pointing true north, guiding him to do the right thing. Braddock was a prideful man, and the idea of having to rely on charity to feed his family was humiliating. So as soon as he started earning money again, he redeemed himself by returning the money that was never his in the first place.

When Social Security, unemployment benefits, and welfare were first introduced in the U.S. during the Great Depression, unemployed workers, like my parents and James J. Braddock, didn't want a government *handout*—they wanted a *hand up*... they wanted opportunities... they wanted jobs... they wanted to pay their own freight. They were ashamed to take money from the government and took any job they could to earn money so they could avoid the humiliation of having to take charity.

But today, people have become so disoriented by political pollution that they think getting freebies from the government is not only acceptable, it's the smart thing to do... the right thing to do... the *only* thing to do. Voters are so deluded by dependence that they have convinced themselves that the government *owes* them a living.

In the Age of Entitlements, pride has been replaced by presumption.

The Opposite of Braddock

To illustrate just how delusional some people have become, I'd like to tell you a story that appeared in the *Tampa Tribune* in early 2010. The story concerned the plight of Angel Adams, a 37-year-old single mother who, along with her 12 school-age children, was being evicted from a small, dingy hotel for failing to pay rent. The 12 children with Adams were the youngest of her 15 children from three different fathers (she had three other children who turned 18 and were on their own). Adams complained to a reporter that she was homeless and hopeless through no fault of her own.

"Nobody's helping me. I'm doing this all by myself," she wailed.

When a caseworker arrived and asked Adams if she had money or a job, Adams replied, "This is my job. This is my work. I need money. I need transportation. My children need a place to live."

Later in the day the regional director of the Florida Department of Children and Family Services (DCFS) paid Adams a visit and offered Adams a cottage large enough for her and the children. Adams reluctantly agreed to take it. You see, Adams didn't trust the DCFS. A child protection team removed her kids from her two years previous, and Adams only got them back six months prior to the newspaper article.

"My family has been railroaded," she lamented. "Someone needs to pay." One person who can't pay is Gerry Brown, the father of 10 of the children. Brown is currently serving a five-year prison sentence for selling cocaine.

Depressing, isn't it, that someone could be so delusional as to blame a government agency for problems she created herself, and then have the

24

gall to demand the government fund, feed, and house her and her children? Meanwhile, taxpayers are on the hook for Angel Adams' choices. The sad part is, when her boyfriend gets out of prison, there may be more children on the way.

"I can have as many as I want to. All my children are a gift from God," Adams said. True. But because of her misguided mindset, millions of responsible people who work and pay taxes, including me, are picking up the tab for her "gifts."

Dependence leads to delusion, indeed.

Adams Nurtured by Culture of Dependency

Adams is an exaggerated example of how dependence leads to delusion. The fact that Adams has a lot of kids is not the issue here. People have been having large families for thousands of years.

Nothing wrong with that.

What's wrong is Adams' mindset... her conviction that someone other than herself or her family owes her food, shelter, transportation, and spending money. That kind of belief system didn't just pop into her head out of the clear blue sky. Her belief system was planted and nurtured over the years by a Culture of Dependency. Her decision to have 15 kids without any traditional means of support is a *learned behavior.*

Had Adams been born 100 years ago, she may have had 15 children. But I guarantee you she would NOT have had the attitude that "someone needs to pay," with that someone being taxpayer-funded social programs. At the turn of the 20th century, welfare came from the church, the community, and family, not from the government.

As government programs have expanded in countries around the globe, the cultural mindset has gradually shifted from *internal responsibility* (the mental dialog of "me" and "us," meaning family and friends, taking care of our problems), to *external responsibility* (the mental dialog of "they" and "them," meaning the government, solving our problems).

The Culture of Dependency that Adams grew up in... the Culture of Dependency that kept rewarding her with free food and free diapers and free housing and free school lunches... has contributed to Adams' mental delusions that "someone needs to pay."

Her mental dialogue goes something like this: "Hey, *they* are responsible for me and my kids, not me. *They* paid before, didn't *they*? Then *they* need to pay again. Now. And in the future. And in my kids' future. 'Cause that's what *I need*, and that's what *they* do."

The fact that Adams herself should be responsible for paying her own way just never occurs to her. Why would it? It's not part of her culture, a Culture of Dependency that, by the way, she didn't create.

It was a culture she inherited.

Culture of Dependence Spreads to the Private Sector

And the saddest part is, there's a little Angel Adams in all of us, for the more that government does for us, the less we do for ourselves. The more the government acts like a "helicopter parent," hovering over us, treating us like children... giving us lunch money when we're young and retirement money when we're old... bandaging our boo-boos... picking up our messes and doing our dirty laundry—then the longer we remain children and the less we take responsibility for our poor choices.

In the Culture of Dependence, even the private sector looks for the Nanny State to bandage their knees when they stumble and fall: When too-big-to-fail banks lost trillions of dollars in the recent recession from making too many bad loans and too many risky bets in the stock market, they expected the government to bail them out for their bad choices—*and the Nanny State did!*

When centuries-old car makers—like GM and Chrysler—which have been turning out too many poorly built cars and giving too many concessions to too many union workers for too many years, got caught in a downturn with too much inventory and too little cash reserves, they expected the government to bail them out for their bad choices—*and the Nanny Sate did!*

When the biggest insurance company in the world, AIG, wrote hundreds of thousands of unregulated, off-the-books insurance-type contracts that blew up in their faces, they ran to the government asking for $180 billion to cover the losses from their bad choices—*and the Nanny State did*!

Truth is, the more that government provides a backstop for our poor choices, then the more we'll keep on making poor choices. It doesn't take a genius to understand why household savings rates in the U.S. were much higher prior to the introduction of Social Security—why save for retirement if the government will send you monthly checks starting at age 62?

So, it's not hard to figure out why today, American's dependence on government is, according to *The Heritage Foundation*, "... 14 times higher than in 1962."

Dependence Increasing around the Globe

The U.S. and Europe aren't alone in creating a Culture of Dependency... they're just leading the way. Japan, for example, has been stuck in a recession for nearly 20 years, caused largely by too much government debt and an aging population that is dependent on overly generous government pensions and increasing costs of healthcare. By 2025, economists project that 70% of Japan's annual budget will be spent on social security and interest payments on the national debt.

Virtually every industrialized nation around the globe is facing similar challenges—too many politicians promising too many social programs that cost too much and too many citizens voting to trade their individual independence for the collective dependence on the Nanny State.

Now, don't get me wrong—I want to help people down on their luck... and I don't want to turn my back on old people. But common sense will tell you that governments can't keep spending more than they take in year after year after year. That kind of behavior will get you votes in the short term, but bankrupt in the long run.

Biggest Downsides to Dependence

For governments, the biggest danger to managing the Culture of Dependence is the strain on federal budgets and the burden of paying for outsized national debts. As David Walker, former U.S. government comptroller, observed, "At all levels, government has grown too big, promised too much, and waited too long to restructure."

Europe shows what happens when entitlements are too big and too expensive to afford—but also too entrenched to reform. The benefactors of government giveaways take to the streets with protests, riots, and arson. So, to avoid civil strife, governments keep piling on the debt... keep kicking the can down the road until they're forced to either cut spending or default on their debts.

Bankruptcy is rare among governments. But it does happen.

Three countries have been forced into bankruptcy since 2000— Argentina in 2001, Iceland in 2008, and Ecuador twice in the last decade. And an unexpected downturn in the global economy could force four or five European countries to throw in the towel.

For individuals, the biggest dangers posed by the Culture of Dependence are mental and emotional, as dependence saps initiative and induces "failure to thrive," a medical condition common to elderly people who have lost their independence due to disease or dementia. In essence, failure to thrive is a state of progressive deterioration. Symptoms are impaired coping skills... diminished resilience... and an inability to deal with everyday challenges and bounce back from adverse events.

Impaired coping skills and diminished resilience—sounds a lot like Angel Adams, doesn't it? And it also sounds like millions of other people across America, Europe, Asia, Australia, and Africa who expect the government to ride in on a white horse and save them when, for example, they haven't saved enough for retirement.

Or haven't paid off their credit card debt.

Or haven't stopped smoking cigarettes.

Or haven't upgraded their skills so they can earn a living in a 21st century hi-tech world.

Or haven't committed themselves to replacing bad, non-productive habits with good, life-enhancing habits.

Or haven't read a book since high school.

Or haven't gone to a doctor for their annual checkup in a dozen years.

Unfortunately, dependence has made people so delusional that they expect the government to take care of all their needs and then blame them when the inevitable catastrophe hits in the form of natural disasters, such as Katrina in New Orleans and earthquakes in Japan and Haiti; or in the form of economic disasters, like the near meltdown of the global financial system in late December 2007.

The Government Give Away Car Is Braking to a Stop

We've been heading in the direction of dependence since the 1930s, and now it's time to make a U-turn and head in the opposite direction. As President Reagan famously said, *"We, the people, are the driver. The government is the car."*

Well, the government car has been driverless for far too long, careening downhill, gathering speed, and heading toward a steep cliff. It's time we jumped back in the driver's seat… hit the brakes on entitlement spending… and steered the car back in the other direction toward independence.

Despite political promises, all highways don't run downhill.

I can't promise the road to independence will always be a smooth ride.

But I can promise you it will be worth the trip.

How to Make Every Day Independence Day

Learn to Love a Life of Independence

Learn to Love a Life of Independence

The best place to find a helping hand is at the end of your own arm.

—Swedish proverb

Born into slavery, Aesop, the author of the oft-repeated *Aesop's Fables*, earned his freedom as a reward for his intelligence and insight into human nature. His most famous fables, such as *The Tortoise and the Hare* and *The Ant and the Grasshopper*, have been told and retold, handed down from generation to generation, for more than 2,000 years.

But one of his least-repeated fables, *The Dog and the Wolf*, was likely Aesop's personal favorite, for it recalls his life as a slave while illuminating the price a person pays for living a life of dependence. Its message is as timely today as it was 20 centuries ago when Aesop first told it:

The Dog and the Wolf

A gaunt wolf was almost dead with hunger when he happened to meet a well-fed housedog that was passing by.

"Ah, cousin," said the dog. "Your irregular life will soon be the ruin of you. Why do you not work steadily, as I do, and get your food regularly given to you?"

"I would have no objection," said the wolf, "if I could only get a place such as that."

"I will arrange that for you," said the dog. "Come with me to my master and you shall share my work."

So the wolf and the dog walked toward the town together. On the way there, the wolf noticed that the hair on the back and sides of the dog's neck was worn away, so he asked him how that had come about.

"Oh, it is nothing," said the dog. "That bare spot is where the collar is put on at night to keep me chained up. It chafes a bit, but you soon get used to it."

"Is that all?" asked the wolf. "Then goodbye to you, dog."

The moral: *Better to starve free than to be a fat slave.*

Which Collar Are You Wearing?

Thankfully, the type of *involuntary servitude* that was commonplace in Aesop's time has been outlawed for years, but today most people, like the dog in the fable, submit to wearing a collar of *voluntary servitude* in exchange for steady work and a steady paycheck.

In fact, most humans voluntarily wear many types of collars. Here are just a few of the collars that people put on each day that, in the words of the dog, "chafe a bit, but you get used to it."

The collar of a job we aren't passionate about...

The collar of a demanding boss...

The collar of a time clock...

The collar of a ceiling on your salary...

The collar of credit card debt...

The collar of a big monthly mortgage...

The collar of little or no savings...

The collar of underfunded retirement accounts...

All of these collars rub people the wrong way, but in a Culture of Dependence, people assume that everything in life comes with a collar. A small percentage of independence-loving people, however, live their lives like Aesop's wolf, refusing to fall for the Faustian bargain of trading their life of independence for dependence on others.

Owning Your Own Life

I know all about voluntary servitude. Before moving to Tampa in 1986, I was dependent on a job in Springfield, Illinois, where, for 16 years, I taught English at Southeast High School. For the first few years out of college, I loved teaching. Loved the kids. Loved talking about books and writing. Loved coaching.

Then gradually, as I got older, I began to resent the restrictions on my freedom. You see, as a teacher, someone other than me was always calling the shots in my life. The superintendent told me what school I would teach in... the principal told me what room I would teach in... the department head told me what classes I'd teach... and the students told me I didn't know what I was talking about.

I was tired of doing the bidding of others. Tired of taking orders. Tired of being treated like a child. So, I resigned and headed to Florida to pursue my dream of owning my own life by owning my own business. I started five different businesses in the first two years; three failed. But the other two businesses—writing and real estate—worked out so well that after 20-plus years, I'm still actively writing and publishing books and buying and renting real estate. I couldn't be happier. I set my own hours... pick my own projects... and, yes, own my own life.

I'm debt free and boss free. And loving every minute of it.

Independence is everything I expected—and more. More time for what I want to do. More money than I could have ever made teaching. More control over my work and my life. More rewards and recognition than I ever thought possible. And, most of all, *more self respect*, because I chose to remove the collar of dependence and learned to love, and live, a life of independence.

Climbing the Pyramid to Independence

If you've ever taken a psychology class, you've likely heard of Abraham Maslow, the psychologist who developed a theory he called the "hierarchy of needs."

In short, his theory of needs is shaped like a pyramid, with the base consisting of the most basic physical needs, such as the need for shelter, air, food, and water. Once those needs are met, humans are free to work their way up the pyramid from physical needs to psychological needs. His five-level pyramid looks like this:

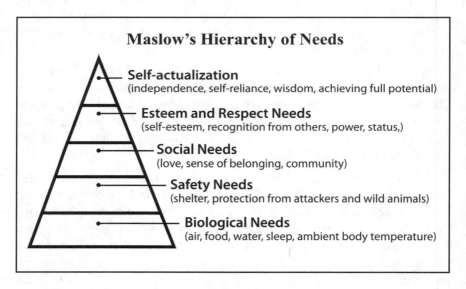

Maslow's Hierarchy of Needs

Self-actualization
(independence, self-reliance, wisdom, achieving full potential)

Esteem and Respect Needs
(self-esteem, recognition from others, power, status,)

Social Needs
(love, sense of belonging, community)

Safety Needs
(shelter, protection from attackers and wild animals)

Biological Needs
(air, food, water, sleep, ambient body temperature)

To get to the top level of the pyramid, self-actualization (which, Maslow said, was the ultimate desire of every human), people have to first travel through the four lower levels. Maslow describes self-actualization as the top level of psychological development, the stage in life where people maximize their inborn talents and abilities and realize their full potential. To become self-actualized, according to Maslow, is to keep growing as a person until you become "fully human," evidenced by independence, autonomy, self-assurance, and the ability to resist outside pressures.

I'm going to one-up Maslow and add another "need" to the top level of self-actualization—*the need for self-employment.*

Self-Employment = Self Actualization

When you think about it, what self-actualization boils down to is owning your own life, wouldn't you agree? Look again at Maslow's criteria for a self-actualized person: *independence... autonomy... self-assurance... the ability to resist outside pressures.*

Sounds like a description of self-employment to me—calling your own shots. Being your own boss. Shaping your own destiny.

In my view, self-employment and self-actualization go together like a horse and carriage—you can't have one without the other. Truth is, unless an employee is part-owner of a company or has a sizeable equity position, they can't really be independent, self-assured, or resistant to outside pressures because with the stroke of a pen on a pink slip, employees can be employed one day, and unemployed the next.

For example, up until the fall of 2008, Lehman Brothers was the oldest and fourth-largest investment bank in the world. Lehman Brothers had survived the Civil War, two world wars, and the Great Depression. But in 2002, Lehman's leadership team began making huge leveraged bets that subprime mortgages would continue to go up, and when the housing bubble burst in 2007, Lehman couldn't cover their losses. On September 15, 2008, Lehman Brothers declared bankruptcy. The stock dropped from a high of $85 to 5 cents, and 25,000 people not only lost their jobs, but also lost all the money they had invested in Lehman stock held in their company 401(k) retirement plans.

Here's my point: I expect some people working for Lehman Brothers in the fall of 2008 considered themselves self-actualized. Many of the long-time employees owned thousands of shares of Lehman stock in their 401(k) accounts. Then, on September 15, they showed up to work like usual, only to be instructed by a squadron of security guards to pack up their belongings and go home. No two-weeks' notice. No paycheck. No severance pay. No gold watch. Just a cardboard box to toss their personal belongings in and a swift kick out the door.

Put yourself in the shoes of one of those Lehman employees: Do you think you'd feel self-actualized—feel *independent, self-assured,* and *in charge of your own destiny*—when the job you thought was secure… when the company stock you thought would fund a worry-free retirement… is gone in the time it takes for a child to blow out a birthday candle?

Poof. Your dreams, gone up in smoke, because your livelihood and your family were *dependent* on the decisions of a boardroom of bankers—your bosses—blinded by the greed of a few top executives, led by CEO Richard Fuld, who paid himself $500 million in the years leading up to the bankruptcy and authorized $20 million in bonuses to three departing executives only four days before filing for bankruptcy!

And to think that 25,000 Lehman employees *depended* on Fuld to make the key decisions that would affect their livelihoods… their futures… *their families.* If that's not delusional thinking, I don't know what is.

Independence: The Invisible Gorilla in Our Lives

Were Lehman employees truly self-actualized?

In a word… No.

Self-deluded? Yes.

Don't get me wrong—I'm not trying to kick ex-Lehman employees while they're down. I'm only using them as an example of what can happen when people become dependent on someone else for their sole source of income… or for their sense of value as a person.

But in the Culture of Dependence, that's what people are taught to do… that's what we tell our children to do—go to school, make good grades, get a good job, and get a paycheck for the privilege of building someone else's dream.

Thanks, but no thanks.

Truth is, we've been taught to look for the wrong things. We get so focused on the second level of Maslow's pyramid—so focused on the need for the safety and security of a paycheck—that we jump off the up escalator and stay stuck on the lower levels. People are so focused on obtaining security that they can't see the top of the pyramid. They've kept their head down so long they don't even know the top level of self-actualization even exists.

It reminds me of a famous psychological experiment called "The Invisible Gorilla," conducted by two college professors at Harvard University. A group of students were asked to watch a one-minute video in which six people—three in white tee shirts and three in black tees—passed two basketballs to each other in a narrow hallway. The viewers were asked to count silently the number of passes the players in white shirts made to each other. The students in the video are moving around randomly while they pass the balls, so viewers are forced to concentrate on the members of the white team as they swirl around tossing and bouncing the ball back and forth. About 20 seconds into the video, someone in a gorilla suit walks into the middle of the action, faces the camera, thumps his chest, and then walks out on the other side. The gorilla is in the video a total of nine seconds.

When the video is finished, the professors asked the viewers if they saw a gorilla in the video. Amazingly, the viewers were so focused on counting the number of passes that half the viewers didn't notice the gorilla! It was as though the gorilla was invisible. (To see the experiment for yourself, go to *theinvisiblegorilla.com*.)

Open Your Eyes to Independence

In the Culture of Dependence, it's easy to get so focused on the bouncing ball of security and what it can provide for us that we miss the gorilla of independence strolling in and out of our lives every day. Although the gorilla is invisible to most people, they still *sense he's somewhere in the room*, even when they won't openly acknowledge his presence.

Why do I say that? Because of another psychological state called "cognitive dissonance," fancy terminology describing that uncomfortable feeling we get when we try to balance two conflicting ideas at the same time. In the hierarchy of needs, people seek security, and they sacrifice to retain it. But they also know deep inside that security is a step up the ladder of fulfillment, but not the top rung.

So, although they may *feel* safer and more secure, they long for something deeper and more fulfilling, even if they can't put their finger on it. That tension between what people *settle for* and what they *truly long for* in their lives creates cognitive dissonance. And no matter how much we try to ignore dissonance or deny it or bury it under a mountain of things, the dissonance remains until we change our attitudes and actions.

People who are not self-actualized feel incomplete... feel like something is missing... feel like there has to be more to life than just security... they feel on edge... a bit off balance... lacking in something... tense... anxious... in short, restless, as if they have a psychological itch they can't scratch.

I know that feeling of restlessness... the feeling that something is missing in my life... a growing dissatisfaction and a yearning to dream a bigger dream and chase after it, instead of settling for the current reality of underachievement.

Been there. Felt that. And then did something about it.

In the Culture of Dependence, there are lots of people who feel unfulfilled. Off kilter. But they're so addicted to depending on someone outside themselves—an employer or the government or permanent disability or a pension or Social Security—that they're afraid to look up for fear they'll see the gorilla of independence pacing in their living room, and that would mean they'll have to DO something about it.

What most people DO, unfortunately, is to act like the viewers of the video counting bouncing balls by counting the little *things* in their lives (their TVs and iPods and smartphones) *as a substitute for counting the single one biggest need that means the most to people—independence.*

The First Step Is Recognition

Perhaps you're experiencing cognitive dissonance in your life... a dissatisfaction you can't quite put your finger on... a void in your life that more security and more things can't fill up.

I suspect that void is a longing for independence... a longing to own your own life by owning your own business. To determine if you have a

40

longing for independence in your life, answer the following questions:

Have you ever wanted to be your own boss?

Would you like to set your own hours?

Are you open to new opportunities and experiences?

Would you be willing to change careers if it meant you would be the president and CEO of your own company?

Do you like to learn?

Would you be open to starting a new business on the side?

Are you self-motivated?

Would you like to have more money for retirement?

Are you a goal setter? If not, would you be open to setting short-term and long-term goals for your life?

Do you have a lot more potential than you're currently using?

Do you feel you have so *much more to offer* yourself... your family... and the world?

If you answered YES to most of these questions, I think you're ready, perhaps even longing, to climb the pyramid to the top and claim your independence. Turn the page to start learning how.

Embrace Entrepreneurship

Embrace Entrepreneurship

The most valuable 100 people to bring into a deteriorating society would not be 100 chemists, or politicians, or professors, or engineers. But rather 100 entrepreneurs.

—Abraham H. Maslow

America can't take credit for starting entrepreneurship—free trade and family-owned businesses had flourished throughout Europe, Asia, and Africa for centuries before the Pilgrims settled the Plymouth Colony in 1620.

But the Pilgrims deserve credit for instituting a system we now call free enterprise to the New World—a system that creates financial freedom by rewarding self-interest and self-reliance.

Here's the fascinating story of how free enterprise saved a failing colony and changed the world

From Communism to Capitalism

For the first two years of the Plymouth Colony's existence, the leaders established a communist system of farming, reasoning that equal sharing was what God wanted. All of the male adults farmed together, and whatever they produced was locked in a storehouse. An equal portion of food was rationed to each adult regardless of their contribution to the harvest.

The colonists who worked hardest were given the same ration as the ones who lay under shade trees complaining they were too sick or weak from hunger to work. Women and children stayed out of the fields, complaining farming was meant solely for the men.

The communist system was a bust. Not surprisingly, their harvests were meager. (If complaints and excuses were seeds, this system would have had a bumper crop.) And though deeply religious, the colonists started stealing from each other. The first two years brought famine and near starvation for the entire expedition. The leader, Gov. William Bradford, wrote, "... famine must surely ensue next year also if not some way prevented."

Famine was not only prevented but abundance ensured when the leaders, after much debate, set up a new system for farming. Instead of communal farming, each family was assigned a parcel of land and whatever each family produced was theirs to keep.

Bradford observed an immediate change early in the planting season.

"The women now went willingly into the field, and took their little ones with them to set corn," he wrote in the spring of 1623. Adults who alleged weakness and sickness the prior planting season were suddenly reenergized, and in the fall, the family plots were so bountiful that the colonists traded excess food with fellow settlers and local Indians for wild game, blankets, and tools.

Learning the Lessons from Two Modern-day Nations

The Pilgrims learned the hard way a basic truth of human nature—people tend to work harder and produce more when they own what they produce. No big surprise there. That's the way we humans are wired. Free enterprise freed the Pilgrims to pursue their own best interests, and in doing so, transformed crop production from scarcity to surplus in just one growing season.

Switching from a communist system to a capitalist system worked wonders for the pilgrims' prosperity, and the lesson learned by a simple, 100-person community back in 17th century applies to complex national economies in the 21st century: *Discourage dependence* on the government and *encourage independence* through entrepreneurship, and economies will flourish.

The recent deaths of two national leaders, Vaclav Havel, the first president of the Czech Republic, and Kim Jong Il, the supreme leader of North Korea, illustrates the stark contrast between capitalism and communism in today's world.

Both men grew up indoctrinated in communist ideology at a young age, but the similarity ends there. Kim chose to retain the top-down, totalitarian system of government founded by his father in 1948, imposing his supreme control over 20 million people by making them completely dependent on the state for employment, food, and shelter.

The democratically elected Havel, on the other hand, resented government intrusion in citizens' lives and legislated independence at every opportunity, privatizing government-run businesses and eliminating laws that restricted free enterprise. The results were predictable: In two decades, Havel helped the Czech people unleash an economic boom unequaled in Eastern Europe. By the time of Havel's death in 2011, the Czech per capita GDP would grow five times larger than in 1990.

Compare the economic miracle of the Czech Republic to the economic disaster of North Korea, which shows as a black spot on the night view of Google Earth, the result of rampant electrical shortages. Mismanagement of collective farms has led to massive shortages of food, resulting in half the children malnourished and 25% underweight (except for the offspring of high-ranking officials in the Communist Party, who appear healthy and well fed).

What Is Entrepreneurship?

I get the feeling that most people think of entrepreneurs as an exclusive club reserved for boy-geniuses like Steve Jobs and Bill Gates and Mark Zuckerberg. But entrepreneurship isn't solely limited to one-in-a-billion prodigies. It's available to anyone living in a country that promotes and protects free enterprise.

"Two hundred years ago, essentially all workers were entrepreneurs," says Tim Kane, Ph.D. in economics and founder of two software companies. "Most were small farmers, and there was no legal distinction between working as an employee or an independent contractor."

The word *entrepreneur* derives from the French word for enterprise, and Webster defines an entrepreneur as "a person willing to launch a new venture and accept full responsibility for the outcome."

Nothing elitist about that definition, is there?

Even today, entrepreneurship is the province of ordinary, everyday people who decide to own their own lives by owning their own businesses. No need to be a genius to do that—just a desire to commit to a life of independence based on your own efforts and abilities, rather than depending on someone else for a paycheck.

Entrepreneurs start all kinds of businesses and come in all ages: The mid-thirties married couple from Brazil who clean my house... the 40-year-old guy who mows my lawn and trims my hedges... the 68-year-old guy who renovates the foreclosed condos I buy... the 50-year-old woman who cuts my hair once a month... the married couple who own the independent insurance agency that insures my income properties— all these people are entrepreneurs who started their careers working for someone else until they decided to strike out on their own. As business owners, they work hard, set their own hours, own their own homes, and, most importantly, own their own lives. That's the American Dream, and it's available to anyone living in a free-enterprise zone with the vision to see it and the drive to make it happen.

Three Types of Entrepreneurs

During my business career, I've observed three types of entrepreneurs: *intentional* entrepreneurs... *reluctant* entrepreneurs... and *accidental* entrepreneurs.

In fact, I've been all three types at one time or the other since I was 30 years old, when I bought my first investment property, a four-unit apartment building in Springfield, Illinois. In that case, I was (and still am) an **intentional entrepreneur**. Over the years I've bought and sold more than a dozen investment properties worth several million dollars. My current plan is to own five to 10 condominiums near my home in Tampa and use the rental income as one of my four streams of revenue.

In 1992, I became a **reluctant entrepreneur** when I was forced to open a newsletter writing business after I was fired as a technical writer documenting a software program for Verizon. Six weeks into the Verizon job, I got fired—and for good reason. I was a good writer but a lousy technician. I didn't know software from tableware, so it was a bad fit.

At the time I was devastated by the firing, but it freed me to pursue more generalized writing, which is a much better fit for my skill set and led to my writing and editing 25 books that have sold more than 5 million copies in the years since my manager at Verizon told me to pack up my belongings and escorted me out the front door. Ironically, he did me perhaps the biggest favor of my life, releasing me from a job I wasn't suited for so that I could become a well-compensated business owner instead of a poorly paid employee.

Within a year of my firing, I became an **accidental entrepreneur** when I was introduced to a young sales trainer named Burke Hedges. Burke encouraged me to write video scripts and personal growth books, and we eventually became partners in a successful publishing company and worked together for nearly 20 years.

The Power of the Two 'O' Words

To become a successful entrepreneur, it doesn't matter if you pursue entrepreneurship or you stumble into it or you're pushed into it—all that matters is that you're motivated by two "O" words—**opportunity** and **ownership**.

If your heart and mind are *open to opportunity...* and if you have a deep-seated need to *own your own life...* then you have the building blocks for becoming an entrepreneur and living a life of independence. Everything else can be learned.

But some people wouldn't know an opportunity from an opossum. And others run from ownership as if it were a swarm of angry African bees, preferring instead to place their faith, and fate, in someone else's hands. That's fine if some people prefer employment to ownership—each to his own. But don't ask me, an *independent* owner of two profitable businesses, to pay more taxes so that *dependent people* can extend their unemployment checks after they get laid off from their job.

People who choose dependence must live with the consequences, just as I have to live with the consequences when there is a downturn in one of my businesses. And believe me, I've seen downturns—big ones! But a *downturn* is better than *down and out,* which is what dependent people become when they lose their jobs and can't find another one for months, perhaps years.

Why Entrepreneurship Is on the Wane

The world is seeking a rebound from the Great Recession of 2008, but it's slow in coming. Given the always-on connectivity of the Internet and ubiquitous smartphones and the breathtaking pace of innovation, entrepreneurship should be expanding and pulling us out of the worst economy since the Great Depression.

But, ironically, the rate of entrepreneurship is declining. According to recent research, entrepreneurship in the U.S. and developed nations has been flat for decades. Something is holding back self-starters. What gives? Stirred by the media and pandering politicians who talk endlessly about the need for more jobs, jobs, jobs, *people are falling for wishful thinking,* buying into the myth that they can land a safe and secure job with benefits and a nice pension... you know, the kind of lifetime employment their grandparents enjoyed.

In other words, most people would rather *depend on a boss* than *depend on themselves.* Why? Because people have been taught to be dependent on jobs or the government. Laid-off workers are sitting around collecting unemployment checks for a year or more, waiting for the economy to rebound so someone will hire them instead of hiring themselves as CEO of their own startup enterprise. Most people who grow up in developed countries have jobs all their lives, so they think that is the only "safe" way to create wealth.

Most immigrants, on the other hand, don't come from countries offering good-paying jobs and unemployment benefits, so they come looking for the two Os—*opportunity* and *ownership*—instead of automatically seeking dependence on a job. According to the Kauffman Foundation, immigrants are 30% more likely to form new companies than are native-born citizens. Ebay, Google, and PayPal were all co-founded by immigrants.

Risky Business vs. Risky Employment

Most people perceive entrepreneurship as too risky... that there's no guarantee of success, so it's safer to settle for a job (even a job you hate—at least it's a job!). Well, that's what I feel about jobs today—they're *too risky*! In today's work environment, you can be hired one day, fired the next.

Okay, I'll admit that in the 1950s and even through the '60s and '70s, companies had a sense of obligation to their employees. Even Fortune 500 companies preferred taking losses to making layoffs... they provided generous pensions... they took pride in offering lifetime employment... they placed the happiness of their employees above happiness of the shareholders.

Those days are dead and gone—forever—killed by cutthroat competition... buried by globalization... and eulogized by mutual-fund managers desperate to wring out every penny of profit in the stock market. Yet, despite the risky employment environment, the myth of the "secure job" continues to lure people to dependence on a boss and a paycheck.

The Art of the Deal

"All human beings are entrepreneurs," said Nobel Peace Prize-winner Muhammad Yunus, the economist who started the microcredit movement in his native Bangladesh. His loans have helped hundreds of thousands of people too poor to qualify for traditional bank loans to lift themselves out of poverty by starting home-based businesses.

Yunus is right—deep inside, we're all entrepreneurs. How else do you explain the explosion of activity on Ebay and Craigslist... the popularity of flea markets... the proliferation of garage sales and craft shows on weekends? Anyone selling or swapping goods and services online or on the ground is exercising their inner entrepreneur. Why would someone give up their weekends to make a few bucks? The profit motive, of course. But owning a business and working that business is about more than just making money. Business is its own reward. It's fun. It's satisfying. It's invigorating. It's productive. It's meaningful. It gets our juices flowing... gets the brain working and the blood pumping.

Think of it this way. People are reluctant to part with their hard-earned money. That's understandable. So when you own a business that provides a product or service that people are willing to hand you their money for... well, it's the ultimate validation that you're doing something good and useful.

The famous pop artist Andy Warhol earned tens of millions selling his paintings and prints, and he equated entrepreneurship to art: "Being good in business is the most fascinating kind of art," quipped Warhol. "Making money is art and working is art and good business is the best art of all."

So, get started creating the best art of all—your own masterpiece—your own business.

Don't Put Your Keys to Success in Someone Else's Pocket

How to Make Every Day Independence Day

Don't Put Your Keys to Success in Someone Else's Pocket

The basic problem that most people have is that they're doing nothing to solve their basic problem.

—Dr. Norman Vincent Peale

Let's start with a joke:

A clerk, a sales rep, and their department manager are walking to lunch when they find an antique brass lamp. The clerk rubs the lamp to clean it, and a genie pops out.

The genie says, "I'll give each of you just one wish."

"Me first," says the clerk. "I want to be in the Bahamas driving a speedboat without a care in the world."

Poof! She's gone.

"Me next," says the sales rep. "I want to be in Hawaii lying on the beach next to my supermodel girlfriend with an endless supply of pina coladas."

Poof! He's gone.

"Okay, your turn," says the genie to the manager.

The manager says, "I want those two back in the office after lunch!"

Moral of the story: *Always let your boss have the first say.*

Putting an End to Dependency

This humorous story reminds us of the power structure in organizations and the pitfalls of office politics... how saying the wrong thing (even if it's true) at the wrong time to the wrong person in the wrong way can cost you a promotion, or even your job. And turn your life upside down.

I've had jobs where I had to walk on pins and needles... had to measure my words carefully when replying to the most innocent questions because, as Shakespeare put it, "The walls have ears," and I never knew who had my back or who wanted to stab me in the back. Office politics can be brutal, and if you're not good at playing politics, it can be fatal to your career.

My lack of power and office politics are the two main reasons I resigned from teaching to start my own business. I was tired of being pushed around like a pawn on the chessboard by more powerful players—department heads... principals... superintendents—they were in charge of my work life, not me. The older I got, the more I resented giving someone else the power to make major decisions affecting my life. Here I was, 40 years old, and I was allowing other people to own my life. I mean, who better to own my life than me, right? So why was I forfeiting control of my most important possession—my life, my decisions, my fate—to other people?

I was *legally* an adult, but I was voluntarily acting like a sullen teenager, biting at the bit to be on my own but being totally dependent on the *real adults* in my life—the real adults who doled out my monthly allowance via a paycheck... the real adults who told me what to wear and what time to work and when to take my vacations... the real adults with the power to make me or break me.

I felt like a kid still living at home: "My house, my rules," as my dad used to say. I resented being treated like a child, being dependent on others for my income... my work schedule... my happiness. I was getting more resentful by the day, and I was the only one who could change that. It was time I took the keys to my success out of other people's pockets and put them in mine, where they belonged.

So, in 1986, I resigned and moved to Tampa to own my own life by owning my own business. Thus began the happiest, most fulfilling, most productive, and most prosperous years of my life. Since that day when I packed up a U-haul in the rain and aimed the truck south to Tampa, every day has been Independence Day for me—more than 25 years of independence, the best 25 years of my life.

Freedom More Important Than Money

I'm not alone in my desire to make every day of my life Independence Day. Deep down, we all feel that way, and recent research bears this out.

Two psychologists in New Zealand combed through surveys of 420,000 people in 63 countries across four decades to create a "well-being index" to see what made people happy in their daily lives. The researchers discovered that across time, cultures, and countries, people placed independence at the top of their value pyramid, even more highly than money. When asked to describe their most satisfying experience of the past week, month, or year, they never replied, "I got a bunch of money," said a researcher. They said things like, "I did something meaningful that I chose to do, and I did it well."

"Autonomy is really about self-organization and self-regulation and goes to the heart of what a well-lived life is all about," said Kennon Sheldon, a psychologist at the University of Missouri. Because autonomous people function independently without outside control by others, they feel good about themselves. And that makes them happier and healthier in all areas of their lives.

"Countries scoring high in autonomy had less stress, less burnout, less mental health problems, and so on," said psychologist Ronald Fischer. Researchers were surprised to learn that money played not the lead role in happiness, but a supporting role. In other words, money only makes people happier when it enhances their sense of freedom. More money gives you more control over your life and your choices, which, in turn, makes you happier.

We've all heard a thousand times the old expression, "Money can't buy happiness." And it's true. Money can't buy happiness when people spend it to buy things. If a person has a hole in their soul, they can't fill it with material *things* no matter how many toys they have or how much they cost. But *money can buy happiness when people spend it to buy more independence*, such as using your savings to pave the way to independence by opening your own business.

That's what I did back in the 1980s, which is why I've long understood that money is freedom.

Freedom from a boss.

Freedom from having to do mundane, time-consuming chores—like washing the car or mowing the lawn—which leaves more time to be more productive to make more money to buy more freedom.

Freedom to schedule your work around your lifestyle, instead of your lifestyle around your work.

Freedom to put the keys to success in your own pocket, instead of having to sit in the back seat while someone else drives your life.

What Happens When Poppa Can't Pay Anymore?

What happens when people compromise their independence by turning their backs on free enterprise in favor of the "guarantee" of a free lunch, only to learn that the provider of that lunch (it could be the federal government or the state or the province or the municipality or Enron or General Motors or name-your-business) has so many dependents on the payroll or pensions that it can't pay its bills anymore?

The answer: It ends in tears… or teargas when angry, dependent people riot in the streets, as is happening in Greece. To get more loans to keep the country running, the Greek government agreed to lay off half a million public employees and cut the minimum wage and pensions by 20%.

With unemployment running at a staggering 50% among workers 25 and younger, little wonder, then, why 100,000 protestors stormed Athens, some tossing firebombs at police and torching banks and businesses. That's what happens when overspent governments make promises they can't keep.

In an article for *Vanity Fair* magazine, financial expert Michael Lewis describes what created the crisis in Greece this way: "As it turned out, what the Greeks wanted to do with a pile of borrowed money [in the form of government bonds] was turn their government into a piñata stuffed with fantastic sums and give as many citizens as possible a whack at it."

It Hurts to Pay the Piper

Look, I'm not picking on Greece—the piñata analogy could just as easily be used to describe most other European countries ... or North America ... or Japan—as politicians bribe taxpayers to vote for them by promising ever-more generous giveaways. Government-backed giveaways and government-backed jobs and government-backed pensions and government-backed healthcare sound great, but here's the catch— *somebody has to pay the government so the government can fund their entitlements.* But when the *takers* of government handouts outspend the *makers* who pay the taxes to the point that the government can't pay back its loans, well, things fall apart fast.

Here's a simple economic truth for everyone who has considered choosing the government's free lunch over free enterprise: *If you don't choose independence on your own terms, eventually, your over-spent government will be forced to choose independence for you.*

At some point, deep-in-debt democracies will have to tighten their belts because they can't borrow forever. When that day comes in one year or five years or 10 years or whenever, everyone dependent on the government for a job... or "free" healthcare... or a pension is going to suffer.

In the coming years, the only people not devastated by government cutbacks in entitlement spending will be people living a life of independence. By necessity, reliance on the government will be replaced by self-reliance.

So I ask you, wouldn't you rather be in a position to choose independence while you can rather than have it forced upon you by a destitute and desperate government? Wouldn't you rather be in a position to be proactive so you could prepare for a new career... do your research... learn a new trade... improve your skill set... or even start your own part-time business?

The other option is to sit with your fingers crossed, waiting for the government (or your employer) to pull the lever and open the trap door under your feet before you're prepared for the drop. What you thought was a safety net under your feet is now a freefall into the deep end of the pool—it's sink or swim and the lifeguard is off duty.

Cuba Pulls Down the Government Piñata

A classic example of this harsh reality is Cuba, which, under strict communist rule since 1959, has demanded that their citizens remain dependent on the government. As a result, virtually every Cuban business, from hamburger stands to shoe repair shops, was nationalized. For five decades it was against the law in Cuba for an individual to own a business or make a profit.

Until recently the government employed 90% of the island's 5 million workers. Despite the fact that buildings were crumbling... manufacturing slowed to a crawl... poverty was increasing... and goods were scarce, the Castro brothers and their military minions adhered to the communist Daddy Daycare playbook: give yourself to the government, and the government will provide.

Then in the fall of 2010, Fidel Castro finally admitted the obvious to a U.S. journalist: "The Cuban model doesn't even work for us anymore," said the 84-year-old retired president (although, to be truthful, the communist model in Cuba never did work).

So, the cash-strapped government did what every Daddy Daycare government must do eventually—they reversed their economic course 180 degrees. "Our state can't keep maintaining bloated payrolls," said a statement from the government union. As a result, the Cuban government announced it's laying off 500,000 state workers and trying to create hundreds of thousands of private-sector jobs in a desperate attempt to shift the nearly bankrupt economy toward a more market-oriented system.

For the first time since 1959, Cubans will be able to sell their services as independent contractors. Accountants, who previously were employed only by the government, can set out on their own. People are free to rent their cars or homes and keep the profits, which will be taxed. And the Central Bank is studying ways to grant small-business loans, which would have been unthinkable a few years ago.

Like I said earlier, if *you don't choose independence on your own terms, eventually, the government will be forced to choose independence for you.* Which is exactly what is happening in Cuba.

Changing Places

Cuba is irrefutable proof that dependence is a disaster waiting to happen because one day, like it or not, the entity you're dependent on— your parents... your employer... your state pension plan... whoever or whatever—won't be around to give you your allowance anymore. And on that day, you'll be forced into living a life of independence, no matter how unprepared you are for the change.

So, here's what amazes me and should spur you to start preparing to live a life of independence. While Cuba tosses in the towel on its economic model, acknowledging that dependence on the government is unsustainable, the *rest of the countries in the West are embracing the Cuban model* of dependence on big government for all your needs by adding government jobs... expanding government healthcare... and increasing government-funded programs, such as food stamps, which increased 70% in the U.S. in only four years to a staggering 45 million people in 2011.

In short, the Cuban economic system that the founder, Fidel Castro himself, has been forced to admit doesn't work and is aggressively trying to disassemble *is the same system democratic governments around the globe are aggressively trying to adopt*!

What's wrong with this picture?

I've Seen This Movie Before

Did we fall down a rabbit hole or is the pull of dependency so strong that the politicians and the people who vote for them can't resist its siren song? It's madness, suicidal madness, for democratic countries that were founded on independence... that flourished because of independence... that fought two world wars and sacrificed millions of lives for independence... to do a U-turn and embrace a failed model based on dependence that we've watched slowly disintegrate for half a century.

I feel like I'm in seventh grade again, watching an old vampire movie with my buddies, screaming at the innocent heroine on the screen not to go near the tall, pale man in the black cape. But she's irresistibly drawn to him, and I cover my eyes as he pulls his cape around her shoulders and lowers his fangs toward her exposed neck as the scene fades to black.

I'm telling you, dependency is a vampire, and it's going for your jugular. So throw open the curtains to let in the daylight and grab a stake while there's still time—you have to slay this monster before it's too late... before it turns you into... *one of them*!

Get Financially Fit

LESSON **6**

Get Financially Fit

*Money is life's fire. It is an excellent servant,
but a terrible master.*

—P.T. Barnum,
American showman

You'll likely remember the media-driven story about Steven Slater,
the Jet Blue flight attendant who, after what he described as an altercation
with rude passengers, abruptly quit his job by exiting his aircraft via the
emergency chute. If your first reaction to Slater's exit was to either laugh
or cheer, or both, you weren't alone—the story hit a collective nerve,
becoming one of the biggest news stories of the year.

What made the story newsworthy for the media was the way Slater
"took the chute" to quit his job—glamorous, creative, dangerous, and
public. But what struck a chord with most people wasn't just HOW he
quit his job, but WHY he quit his job: *to declare his independence* from a
low-paying, high-stress job.

Taking the chute was the sizzle.

But declaring his independence was the steak.

65

We've all fantasized about taking the chute at one time or the other, declaring our independence from a tyrannical boss... a dead-end job... a soulless career... a dying industry. But more often than not, we've stayed longer than we should have because we needed the paycheck.

Slater's impulsive (some would say immature) resignation made him an instant celebrity, but after his 15 minutes of fame was over, what then? Was his exit the beginning of his living a life of independence? Or was it the end of the runway because he didn't lay the groundwork and pave the road that leads away from job dependence ... to financial independence?

5 S's to Successful Independence

In today's volatile global economy, most everyone with a job will take the chute during their working years—and more than likely, it won't be voluntary. Unless you work for the government, job security is a thing of the past—and even government workers are being pushed out in record numbers as budgets tighten and technology replaces the need for human hands.

Truth is, we live in a topsy-turvy world of employment. According to government reports, the average worker will have 10 to 12 different jobs in 5 to 7 different careers by retirement age. Why? Because globalization, innovation, and technology are changing our world in months, instead of decades. The top 10 in-demand jobs in 2011 did not even exist in 2004, according to research by the Sony Corporation. Today we can't rely on a job to provide a steady income and security. Which means today, more than ever, living a life of independence isn't a luxury... it's a necessity.

As I see it, there are 5 steps to living a life of independence. I call them the *5 S's to Successful Independence*:

5 S's for Successful Independence

Step 1) Start with a job

Step 2) Save

Step 3) Spend smart

Step 4) Sideline business

Step 5) Select your retirement

As you can see from the chart below, each one of the S's will move you along a continuum from total dependence... to total independence:

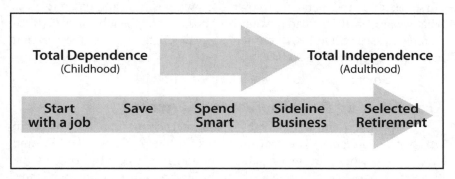

Let's look at each of these five steps to independence in a bit more depth, beginning with *Start with a job*, meaning that working as an employee is a good place to start your working career—but a lousy place to end it.

Step 1: Start with a job:

During the past 20-plus years as an author, I've written frequently about jobs, most always negatively, typically recycling the old job-bashing chestnuts we've all heard time and again: "You know what J.O.B. stands for, don't you?—Just Over Broke."

But as I've gotten older and wiser, I've come to realize that having a job isn't bad. What's bad is *staying in a job* (especially a job you hate) because you're dependent on the paycheck, and you have no other options.

Now, that's bad.

As I see it, working for someone else is a necessary step toward successful independence for most people, just as living with your parents is a necessary stage to prepare yourself for moving out and living on your own. To me, jobs are a means to an end, with the "end" being self-employment and, ideally, financial independence.

Let's face it—few people have the brains to make the leap from being a student to being a CEO of a successful startup company, like Bill Gates starting up Microsoft and Mark Zuckerberg founding Facebook. So, jobs help us make the transition from depending on someone else to give us money in exchange for our time and talents... to eventually positioning ourselves to be independent, to own our own business and pay ourselves what we are worth, instead of what your boss thinks the job is worth (truth is, most bosses will tell you your job is worth less than it is so they can put more money in their pockets).

All the more reason to be your own boss, isn't it?

Transitioning from Employee to Owner

I tell people to think of a job as a paid internship—in a job, you get to *earn* while you *learn*. The "earning" part will help you pay the bills and save money while you grow personally and professionally. But it's the "learning" part that will prepare you for leading a life of independence. In a job, you have the opportunity to learn how to work with others... how to communicate effectively... how to build teams... how to set and achieve goals... how to follow and how to lead... how to motivate teammates... how to make budgets and manage projects... and how to spot opportunities in the marketplace.

A great example of successfully transitioning from dependence on a job to independence as a business owner is Juliet Huck, founder and CEO of TheHuckGroup, a Los Angeles'-based design company specializing in creating visual displays for law firms. Huck was employed as an art director for a big law firm for seven years, learning her craft and saving money to launch her own company. In the final two years as an employee, she worked evenings and weekends to organize and set up her own business so that she could hit the ground running the day she resigned from her job.

In the first seven months in her new business, Huck failed to earn a dime, but she was undeterred. She had a dream and a burning desire to make it a reality. She continued to network, sent out letters and notices to potential clients, and advertised her services on the Web. In her eighth month in business, she landed a $10,000-a-month retainer for producing courtroom displays for a law firm suing a major insurance company. Huck was on her way. Today she employs seven full-time workers and her growing firm bills many millions of dollars a year.

Step 2. Save:

A big key to Huck's success was her discipline to save money from every paycheck when she was working as an employee. Without a nest egg, Huck could never have survived seven months without income.

Look—I'll give it to you straight. You can't be independent without some money in the bank. And the simplest way to make that happen is to save a portion of every paycheck. Unfortunately, the savings rate fell to historical lows during the boom-boom decades of the 1980s and '90s and the years leading up to the Great Recession of 2008. During this time, the historical savings percentage of 12% of gross income per year in the U.S. dropped to *less than zero* for a two-year period, meaning the vast majority of Americans were spending more than they earned, a balloon begging to be popped.

It popped, and the U.S. economy, along with much of the global economy, went flat. Millions lost their jobs, and those with little or no savings teetered on the brink of bankruptcy, or worse, homelessness. Those with savings, on the other hand, were better equipped to deal with the downturn. If people ever needed an incentive to save, the crash of 2008 should do the trick. If that didn't scare people into saving more, then nothing will.

I recommend that people save a *minimum of 20%* of their gross income. When people respond, "I could never live on 80% of my income," my response is, "If you lost your job and got hired at another job paying 20% less, how would you survive?" They usually answer they'd cut back on spending. "Then just pretend you're making 20% less and cut back on those non-essentials," I tell them. "If you took a pay cut, you'd learn to live without the extra money. So, make your own pay cut by paying yourself first with automatic payroll deposit in a savings account." The alternative to saving too little is to be right back rocking the bankruptcy boat in five years when the next recession rolls around.

There are four reasons to save, in the order of importance: Emergency Fund, Investment Fund, Retirement Fund, and Recreation Fund. Let's take a look at each one in a little more detail:

1) **Emergency Fund:** Talk radio host and financial guru Dave Ramsey recommends an emergency fund equivalent to six months of income. He suggests keeping the money in a savings account or CD so that you can access it easily if an unexpected emergency comes up—like loss of a job or a medical crisis.

2) **Investment Fund:** Investments are what I call "spending smart," which I'll talk more about in *Step 3*. Investments are assets that *increase in value*, such as stocks and bonds, rental property, secured loans, or seed money to start a new business. I'm using my investment money, for example, to buy foreclosed condos in Tampa, for as little as $50,000 that sold for $250,000 at the height of the real estate bubble. By buying at rock-bottom prices, I can make 8% to 10% on my investment in rental income, plus enjoy appreciation when the market turns up. I'd also classify money spent on retraining or schooling as an investment, along with a down payment for a home if you can buy in a great neighborhood for a great price and you plan to live there at least 10 years.

3) **Retirement Fund:** The days of dependence on a generous pension to fund your golden years are disappearing as fast as hot dogs at a double-header. I'll talk more about building a retirement fund in *Step 5, Selected retirement*, near the end of this chapter.

4) **Recreation Fund:** Saving for recreation is last in the list because expensive recreations, such as family cruises and trips to Disney World, are indulgences, not necessities. My wife Carol and I, for example, had planned on taking a 10-day trip to London and Paris in the spring of 2011. But when Carol's law firm suspended matching the employees' 401(k) contributions, it meant Carol had to contribute an extra $6,000 from her annual salary to her retirement plan. People who are serious about living a life of independence understand that *retirement trumps recreation,* so we swapped the $8,000 trip to Europe for a $2,000 four-day trip to Miami and

contributed the $6,000 in savings to Carol's 401(k). It was a win/win—we still got our vacation and her 401(k) still got fully funded for the year.

Step 3: Spend Smart:

When it comes to spending, we have two choices:

Spend dumb. Or...

Spend smart.

Spending dumb means buying things that go down in value over time, like new furniture, clothing, and cars. I know, I know—we all need tables and transportation. But we all don't need a new $80,000 Range Rover when a used Toyota SUV with low miles will do the same job for less than one-fifth of the cost. As Robert Kiyosaki says in *Rich Dad, Poor Dad*, "Rich people buy assets. Poor and middle class people buy liabilities and call them assets."

Spending smart means buying *real* assets that go up in value over time, such as real estate (if you buy at the *right time*, in the *right place*, for the *right price*), stocks and bonds, quality art and antiques, collectibles, collateralized loans, and the like.

When it comes to buying real estate, for example, I've long been a proponent of buying the worst house in the best neighborhood and increasing the value by fixing it up. Beginning in 1987, I've bought 14 rundown properties in great neighborhoods in Tampa at way-below-market prices. Once the renovations were completed, I could demand above-market rents and was able to sell eight of my properties at top prices from 2002 to 2006, when the market peaked.

I began buying real estate again in 2009 when a flood of foreclosures became available. Recently, I've been buying condos in a first-class development just minutes from my house for $50,000 or less that sold in 2005 for $200,000-plus. My goal is to own five units that each net me $500 a month, increasing my annual income by $30,000 a year. Hey, real estate works for me, but I understand it's not for everyone. There are just as many ways to spend smart as there are to spend stupid—you just have to be on the lookout for ways to add to your wealth.

Step 4: Sideline Business:

The easiest, least risky way to start on your road to financial independence is to start a sideline business while you're still fully employed. That way you have money coming in while you're building your own business in the evenings and on weekends.

Yep, you're going to have to make some sacrifices. Sideline businesses take time and money. But once you transition from the dependence on a paycheck to the independence of owning your own business—well, I can just tell you the feeling of satisfaction will far outweigh the sacrifice.

When I was 28 years old, I bought my first house for $15,000. The realtor called it a handyman special. My friends called it a dump. I called it my diamond in the rough and went to work shaping it into a little gem. I worked on that house nights and weekends for 18 months. I sacrificed my favorite activity—playing tennis—while I renovated that house, but in the end, it was worth it. I sold it and used the profits to buy my first four-unit apartment building, launching a sideline that has earned me several million dollars over the course of three decades.

Another sideline of mine, writing and editing, enabled me to forge a publishing partnership that resulted in 25 books that have sold 5 million copies worldwide.

I'm not trying to steer you into real estate or writing—there are thousands of business opportunities out there. You just have to be open to them. Thomas Edison summed up opportunity this way: "Opportunity is missed by most people because it is dressed in overalls and looks like work." Both jobs and sideline businesses require work, but only sideline businesses can lead to a life of independence.

Step 5: Select Your Retirement

When people ask me what I do, I say I'm semi-retired: "I plan my work around my golf instead of my golf around my work," I tell them.

And it's true.

I still work and have no plans to ever quit. Why should I? I set my own hours. Choose my own projects. Work only with the people I want to work with. Love what I do. And make a nice living doing it. And I can thank two sideline businesses I started more than 30 years ago for the privileges I enjoy as a result of my choosing to live a life of independence.

Most of my dearest friends are totally retired. When I ask them what they do all day, many say something like, "Oh, I piddle around. Run errands. Stuff like that."

That's what they've *selected for their retirement.* That's fine for them, but as for me, I don't want to spend my final time on earth "piddling." I work because *I want to…* not because *I have to.* I want to create… I want to make things happen… I want to negotiate deals… I want to improve properties… I want to oversee my investments.

Piddle my final days away? No thanks.

My friend Bruce is turning 70 this year. He's survived two heart attacks and prostate cancer, but he's anything but a piddler. He plays golf three days a week, tennis twice a week, and still manages to renovate my condominiums within 60 days of my receiving title. Bruce does the work by himself, everything from demolition to plumbing to electrical to tile work to kitchen cabinets. He's a one-man work crew.

Sit in an overstuffed chair and watch TV all day? Not Bruce. He can't sit still. So, in his retirement, Bruce selects to work all around the neighborhood because he wants to, not because he has to. Work not only gives him extra income but also satisfaction… and a sense of accomplishment… and purpose in his life. His wife Diane works three days a week and has no plans to retire either. "You're either a doer or a don't-er," she says. She's a doer.

Diane and her husband Bruce are financially independent enough that they don't have to work. They could choose to pass their days piddling. But they've selected an active retirement.

Independence Isn't Reserved Just for Retirement, You Know

Can you achieve financial independence in your retirement by depending on a job? Of course. Millions of government employees and state workers retire with comfortable pensions. But they have to trade 40 years of their lives, from ages 25 to 65, dependent on a job to receive their pension.

I, for one, wasn't willing to make that trade-off.

The best decision I ever made was to declare my independence in 1986 when I was young enough to savor all the benefits of owning my own life by owning my own business. And I still do!

If you resolve to incorporate the *5 S's to Successful Independence* into your life, I guarantee that when you're finally in a position to "take the chute," you'll land on your feet... and hit the ground running and jumping for joy!

LESSON 7

Get Physically Fit

How to Make Every Day Independence Day

Get Physically Fit

*It is not the mountain we conquer but
ourselves.*

—Sir Edmund Hillary,
first climber to reach top of Mt. Everest

Skinny and sickly at age 15, Jack described himself as "mean and miserable," a "sugarholic" and "junk-food junkie." He briefly dropped out of high school, just another "punk" on his way to a lifetime of broken dreams.

Then he attended a lecture by a well-known nutrition speaker.

The lecture turned his life around.

Jack stopped eating red meat, sugar, and junk food. He started eating raw vegetables and exercising daily. He attended college, earning a degree as a chiropractor. At age 21, Jack opened the nation's first fitness club... expanded to own and operate dozens of fitness centers across the nation... wrote numerous books... and starred in his own televised fitness program that ran on ABC for 25 years.

He's been called the "Godfather of Fitness."

You likely know him by his full name—Jack LaLanne.

Use It or Lose It

"The only way you can hurt your body is to abuse it and not use it," LaLanne said. He was a living example of how healthy eating and exercise can foster independence and extend lives. He died at age 96 of respiratory failure due to pneumonia, exercising up to the day he was admitted to the hospital, physically and financially independent to the end.

Who wouldn't want to live a full, fit life of independence like Jack LaLanne? Let's face it—you can't be independent if you can't walk a city block without sitting down. The good news is that a healthy, happy LaLanne lifestyle is available to all of us if we would just follow what I call "10 Tips to Getting and Staying Physically Fit."

10 Tips to Getting and Staying Physically Fit

Tip 1: *Don't Diet, Lifestyle-It:* Here's a scary statistic: Almost 75% of healthcare costs in the U.S. stems from chronic diseases, many of which can be prevented by lifestyle choices. Americans are making lifestyle choices, all right, just the wrong ones. They're choosing fast food over fruits and vegetables... couch sitting over exercise... and sugary drinks over water and healthy beverages.

The result? Seven of 10 Americans are classified as overweight and one in five is obese. Nearly 75% of healthcare costs in the U.S. stems from treating chronic diseases, led by type 2 diabetes, which can be prevented by healthier eating and regular exercise.

Think about it—it's nearly impossible for people to lead a life of independence if they're too sick or overweight or out of shape to walk up a flight of stairs.

It's easy to blame growing waistlines (not just in the U.S., but throughout the developed world) on McDonald's, the world's largest fast-food chain. Or Pepsi, the world's largest maker of snack foods and second-largest soda manufacturer. Or TV watching, which is linked to bigger bellies, heart disease, and diabetes, according to the American Medical Association.

But it takes the same effort (and less money) to drive past a McDonald's as it does to steer into the parking lot. Vending machines offer bottled water as well as sodas, and TV remotes have an off button. "Our remedies oft in ourselves do lie," said Shakespeare in *All's Well That Ends Well*. Lives won't end well—and they'll end much earlier—unless people start choosing healthier lifestyles.

We've all heard that diets don't work. More accurately, they work for some people for a while… and then when the poor eating habits return, the weight returns, plus a few extra pounds. Research shows that the obese are more likely to be depressed, to miss school or work, to feel suicidal, to earn less, and to find it harder to marry. On top of that, their healthcare costs more, too.

A few basic changes in lifestyle choices can help people lose weight, keep it off, and be happier in the process.

Tip 2: *Eat Healthier:* Let's spend some time talking about how our eating habits have changed over the years. Just 40 years ago, Americans consumed about 2,000 calories a day. Today that number has spiked to 2,700 a day, a 35% increase. Junk food is certainly one contributor. But the truth is we're just eating more food more often. The best-selling cookbook *The Joy of Cooking* was first published almost 80 years ago. It's in its seventh edition and is still a top seller. Of the 18 recipes that have been continuously published since 1936, the individual serving sizes have increased 63%!

No wonder we're overweight.

Research shows that a Mediterranean diet significantly reduces risk of heart attacks and cancer, the two leading causes of death in developed nations, while also reducing incidences of Parkinson's and Alzheimer's disease.

A Mediterranean diet is primarily plant-based and uses herbs and spices instead of salt for flavoring. Foods to eat are vegetables (raw, steamed, or lightly sautéed) and fruit (but not fruit juice, which contains loads of sugar). Replace red meat with fish rich in omega-3 fatty acids, like salmon, sardines, and mackerel. The Mediterranean diet also allows moderate servings of chicken, eggs, yogurt, and cheeses. For snacks, eat a handful of almonds or walnuts with bits of dried fruit. And load up on beans, which are low in fat and high in protein and fiber, while taking it easy on the whole-grain pasta. Replace the dinner rolls and biscuits with dense and delicious whole grain breads.

The Mediterranean diet is not fat free; it just substitutes the good monounsaturated fats, like olive oil and canola oil, for the artery-blocking trans fats found in cookies, cakes, fast food, and frozen dinners. For those with a sweet tooth, substitute dark chocolate for candy bars and ice cream. Ingredients in dark chocolate activate your good HDL cholesterol while lowering your bad LDL cholesterol. For snacks, substitute apples for crackers from the vending machine. Eating a couple apples a day for six months can reduce your artery-blocking LDL cholesterol by 23%, according to TV Doc and heart surgeon, Dr. Oz.

Coffee drinkers, rejoice—recent studies indicate a couple cups of coffee daily are good for your health. But after your morning coffee, be sure to eat fiber-rich cereal or oatmeal for breakfast. Or eat an egg— hard-boiled or poached. One egg provides 13% of your daily protein requirement and may even help prevent Alzheimer's while protecting the eyes from macular degeneration and UV damage.

Tip 3: *Exercise:* "A bear, no matter how hard he tries, grows tubby without exercise," wrote A.A. Milne, creator of the honey-loving, pot-bellied bear Winnie the Pooh. Dozens of studies show that people who exercise are thinner, happier, healthier, and live longer than those who don't, with reduced chance of heart disease, high blood pressure, stroke, type 2 diabetes, colon and breast cancers, depression, falls, and even mental decline.

At the minimum, walk 30 minutes a day, five days a week. Walking is great, but swimming and biking regularly are even better. People who bike three hours a week, for example, reduce their chances of heart attack and stroke by 50%.

"If you had to pick one thing that came closest to the fountain of youth, it would be exercise," says Stanford University's James Fries, M.D., expert on aging. The American College of Cardiology in New Orleans says that consistent lifelong exercise preserves heart muscle in the elderly to levels that match or even exceed that of healthy young sedentary people. Their studies following both active and sedentary people over many decades show that physical activity preserves the heart's youthful elasticity, whereas among sedentary adults, the size of their hearts shrunk with each passing decade.

For those with desk jobs, at the very minimum, take short breaks of three to four minutes each hour to stand or walk around. People who sit for most of the day are 54% more likely to die of heart attacks than more active types. British researchers found that sitting bus drivers were twice as likely to die of heart attacks as standing trolley operators. At the offices of the magazine *Men's Health*, a few of the most health-compulsive writers don't even have chairs. They write, edit, and answer emails while standing in front of computers all day.

A final thought if you are serious about getting more exercise. You may be better off buying a dog than a gym membership. Researchers in Britain found that people with dogs exercised six hours more per week than those who worked out at a gym. The average dog owner walks his pet more than 30 minutes twice daily and longer on weekends. Those short bursts add up to more than eight hours of physical activity a week!

Tip 4: *Supplement:* "Ideally, we'd get all the vitamins we need from the foods we eat, but few of us actually do," says Dr. Oz in *Parade* magazine. "That's where multivitamins come in. Choose one that supplies 100% of your daily allowance." Harvard Medical School says, "Taking a high-quality multivitamin is a good start toward ensuring that you are getting what you need."

Much research also endorses specific supplementation as needed, including calcium (especially for women), vitamins B6, B12, and folic acid (which become more deficient with age); and vitamins C and D. Research and consumer endorsements also indicate that there are wellness benefits to regular doses of certain protein powders, high-quality fish oil, and phytonutrient supplements.

More and more doctors are recommending supplementation to replace or augment pharmaceuticals, many of which have negative side effects. My personal physician, for example, recommended I take a slow-release iron tablet, folic acid, coenzyme Q-10, and a pharmaceutical-grade fish oil supplement. I've made supplementation along with a high-fiber breakfast sprinkled with fresh berries as part of my daily routine. Must be working—I wear the same waist-size pants as I wore when I graduated from college in 1968.

Tip 5: *Reduce sugar and salt:* In 2010, PepsiCo, Inc. tried to do the right thing and fight the obesity epidemic by making its leading snack brands (Lays potato chips, Doritos, Cheetos, and Tostitos, among others) healthier by reducing salt by 25% and sugar and transfats by 15% by 2015. PepsiCo called their healthier snacks "it's-better-for-you" portfolio. Only problem was consumers preferred the old "it's-worse-for-you" recipes and sales fell. In early 2012, the world's largest snack-food maker renewed its focus on the original recipes, choosing to improve the health of the company's profits at the expense of the health of chip eaters and soda sippers.

Hey, I don't blame PepsiCo for retreating on their commitment to reduce salt and sugar—consumers voted with their pocketbooks and tossed the healthier snacks right out of the grocery aisles. Ultimately, it's up to individuals to make healthier food choices. But be forewarned—sugar and salt are killers.

Let's start with sugar: For each 12-ounce serving of sugar-sweetened soda a person drinks a day, the risk for diabetes increases 15%. In a Harvard study, nurses who consumed two sugar-sweetened beverages a day had a 35% higher risk of heart attack than those who drank less than one a month. Even 100% fruit juice could be bad if you're consuming large quantities. "Added sugars—whether they come from fruit juice concentrates or corn syrup—all have equally adverse effects metabolically," says Harvard researcher Vasanti Malik.

Sugar is bad. Salt may be worse. The sodium in salt attracts and holds water, making the heart work harder and spiking pressure in arteries, contributing to the early onset of arteriosclerosis and increasing the risk of stroke or heart attack. We get most of our salt not from the saltshaker at home but from bread and rolls, fast foods, canned foods, and snacks. The worst consumers of salt are teenagers, who average 3,800 milligrams of sodium a day, more than twice the ideal 1,500 mg.

82

Cutting a little salt helps a lot. If teens cut their salt by just one-half tablespoon a day, the number of young adults ages 12 to 24 with high blood pressure would drop 63%. "That translates to a 9% reduction in deaths by the time these kids turn 50," according to heart specialist Dr. Michael Roizen.

Tip 6: *Monitor your vitals:* When was the last time you took your blood pressure? Or had a physical by your primary physician? Or had your blood and urine tested to check your cholesterol and glucose levels? Here are the baselines cardiologists suggest for optimum heart health:

Total cholesterol less than 200

HDL (good) cholesterol more than 50

LDL (bad) cholesterol less than 100

Triglycerides less than 150

Blood pressure below 120/80

Blood glucose less than 100

Body-mass index (BMI) less than 25

All it takes to monitor your vitals is an annual physical if you're over 50 and a near-painless draw of blood; or a physical once every five years if you're under 50, your BMI is 25 or under, and you're in good health.

Sadly, one in three Americans has high levels of bad LDL cholesterol; and 66% of those with high LDL do little or nothing to lower it. "Bad cholesterol remains out of control in this country," says Thomas Friedan, director of the Centers for Disease Control and Prevention. LDL accounts for most of the body's cholesterol and, along with high blood pressure and smoking, is a major contributor to strokes and heart attacks. Heed the words of Ben Franklin, an independent man who put his own life on the line so that you and I could live a life of independence: "An ounce of prevention is worth a pound of cure."

Tip 7: *Avoid the 7 risk factors:* For decades, global health leaders have focused on ridding the planet of infectious diseases that killed millions each year: thanks to vaccines and medical advances, potentially fatal diseases such as small pox, polio, whooping cough, and tuberculosis are nearly extinct.

Now doctors are turning their attention to what they're calling "a public health emergency in slow motion" brought on by seven bad lifestyle habits that, over time, lead to chronic diseases, namely, cancer, diabetes, and heart and lung disease. These largely preventable diseases account for nearly 66% of deaths worldwide, or about 36 million people each year.

Research from the American Heart Association shows that most 50-year-olds can live another 40 years if they follow the seven secrets to a long life: stay away from cigarettes, stay slender, exercise, eat healthy, and keep cholesterol, blood pressure, and blood sugar in check.

Oh, and let me add one more health "secret" from the dentists—floss daily. Our teeth and gums are the main portals by which germs and bacteria enter our system, which means you can't have a healthy body without having a healthy mouth.

Tip 8: *Take your meds:* By "taking your meds," I mean follow your doctor's orders. If you're young, thin, active, and healthy, taking your meds means to keep doing what you're doing. If you've had some medical issues, as I have recently, it means doing what your doctor tells you to do... even if it hurts.

Taking your meds sounds simple, doesn't it? Yet in a 2010 study sponsored by Aetna Insurance, doctors were stunned to discover that 33% of the 5,855 Aetna members going home after a heart attack failed to fill their prescriptions for well-established drugs to prevent a recurrence of heart trouble *even when the drugs were offered free*!

What's most amazing is that the average age of the patients was 53, which means if they took their free meds and made a few lifestyle changes, these patients could expect to live another 30 years. But for 2,000 of the nearly 6,000 patients, they'd rather risk another heart attack than take their free meds. Unbelievable. Let's get real here—the best healthcare system in the world, no matter how much money we throw at it, can never cure people who prefer to remain enrolled in the "I-don't-care" healthcare system.

Tip 9: *Build a strong social network:* In his book *Blue Zones: Lessons for Living Longer from the People Who've Lived the Longest,*

84

Dan Buettner, *National Geographic* explorer and author, traveled the globe from Costa Rica to Japan to Italy to discover the regions where people live the longest.

He called these areas "Blue Zones," and by comparing the inhabitants' lifestyles, he identified the nine basic behaviors that promote health and longevity. Five of the nine behaviors are physical—move, eat more veggies, take vacations, stop eating when you're full, and drink red wine in moderation. But four of the "Power 9" habits for longevity focused on spiritual and mental behaviors: find your purpose and pursue it with a passion... feed your soul... join a group... and make family a high priority.

In 2009, Buettner teamed with the United Health Foundation to organize the Blue Zones Vitality Project in the town of Albert Lea, Minnesota, population 18,000. The mission of the Vitality Project was to add healthy years to an entire town. The cornerstone of the project was walking groups called *moais*, a Japanese word for a group of people who support one another for life. In Albert Lea, 600 citizens joined walking *moais* during the project, offering encouragement and accountability. By the time the project ended, nearly 3,500 residents participated. Not surprisingly, the life expectancy of participants 65 and older rose by an average of three years, and all participants said they felt healthier, both physically and mentally.

"Members of my *moais* reached out to me immediately," said one newcomer to the town. "We began talking as we walked, and soon we became friends. That experience helped me open up to more people, and my husband and I not only lost weight and dropped waist sizes, our diabetes symptoms disappeared. Now I think of our new town as home."

Tip 10: *Find your motivation:* What motivates me to get off the couch, slip on bike shorts, and pedal for 50 minutes when I could be reading a book or watching a DVD with a bowl of popcorn in my lap?

Two things: habit and vanity. I've enjoyed the habit of exercising since the day I climbed out of the crib. I've played sports all my life, swam daily during summer vacations, started running regularly in college, and played tennis competitively until my hip gave out in my mid-60s. As for vanity, well, I wear the same size pants I wore in college and I refuse, *refuse*, to buy a size larger.

What's your motivation for getting physically fit? Maybe it's playing with the grandkids... dancing at your son or daughter's wedding... looking good for your 20-year or 30-year or 40-year high school reunion... or fighting off type 2 diabetes. The best motivation for you is whatever gets you eating healthier and exercising regularly.

My mom's familiar refrain as she got older was, "I don't want to be a burden to anyone." Continued independence was her ultimate motivation for quitting smoking and losing weight, and to her credit, she was independent until her final days.

So find your motivation for staying healthy. Embrace it. Announce it to anyone who will listen. And then use it to help you make the choices that will contribute to living a life of independence.

Make Technology Your Tool, Not Your Tyrant

Make Technology Your Tool, Not Your Tyrant

I don't believe technology changes us. We choose to be changed by it.

—Genevieve Bell,
Intel executive

"Technology is a double-edged sword," says inventor and futurist Ray Kurzweil. "Technology can help us focus better, or it can flood us with useless distractions."

To illustrate the good edge of the tech sword, Kurzweil talks about his father, a musician. "My father had to spend time raising money to hire an orchestra just to hear his compositions. Now a kid in a dorm room can do that with a synthesizer and a computer." That's the power of technology to save time and money while leveraging talent.

The opposite edge: Tech can just as easily waste people's time, money, and talents. "Is the amount of information instantly available inversely proportional to wisdom?" asks Nicholas Carr in his book, *The Shallows*. "Will the false and trivial overwhelm the true and meaningful?"

Great question that each of us must answer for ourselves: Will you make technology your servant or your master?... Your tool or your tyrant? To answer that, let's take a closer look at both edges of the tech sword—the *harming edge* and the *helping edge.*

The Harming Edge of Tech

Let's start by talking about how tech can be harmful to the most vulnerable population—our children. Just a few years ago, all a kid could do with a cellphone was place a call, which, if you were a parent, was more helpful than harmful. But today, a phone gives your child the opportunity to text, go online without supervision, and send and receive photos. Do you think most kids—your kids—are ready to make the best choices with all those options available?

A 2010 Kaiser Family Foundation study found that students 8 to 18 spend more than seven hours and 13 minutes a day engaged in computers, cellphones, TV, downloaded music, or video games, resulting in a diminished ability to focus on one thing at a time. In a wired world, there's no downtime for children... no time to sit alone in their room... no time to live inside their minds with just their thoughts... no time to figure out for themselves how to fill their time... no time to imagine... no time to create... no time to stare out the window and dream... no time to read a book... no time to write in a journal.

No time, in other words, to develop a sense of self.

"Technology encourages this fantasy among adolescents that they will never have to be alone," says Sherry Turkle, author of *Alone Together.* "But if they don't learn to be alone, they will only know how to be lonely."

As a result of constant connection at an early age, all-powerful peer pressure becomes all the more powerful. School-lunchroom behavior—gossip, breakups, meanness, and attention-getting games—is enhanced and goes on 24/7. "Facebook can be like high school cafeteria on steroids," quips Emily Listfield in *Parade* magazine. Or worse. "We become disinhibited online," says psychiatrist Elias Aboujaoude. "And our meanest traits come out."

Kids have always been mean. But in the Internet Age, especially under the cloak of anonymity, kids are free, even encouraged, to release their darkest, most vile *Lord of the Flies* urges. Because it's easier to target someone for abuse when you don't have to face them, social media sites can lead to cyber-bullying. Same goes for texting, every teen's favorite medium of communication. In fact, by a wide margin, young people prefer texting to talking (even, I've noticed, while sitting at the same table).

The Dark Side of Texting

Some experts worry that texting will impede young people's development of an essential set of communication skills—how to read facial expressions and subtle changes in voices during face-to-face conversations. "There's a big difference between an apology that involves looking in someone's eyes and seeing that they're hurt and typing, 'I'm sorry' and hitting send," Turkle points out in *Alone Together*.

She has a legitimate concern. The average teen spends two hours a day texting, sending more than 50 texts per day, and teenage girls send and receive more than 4,000 texts a month. My college-age daughter, for example, won't answer her phone unless I text her and tell her to pick up. I shouldn't feel offended—she doesn't answer phone calls from her friends, either. "Kids have told me that they almost don't know what they are feeling until they put it into a text," laments Turkle. For an increasing number of kids, texting isn't what you *do*. Texting is who you *are*.

Almost two of every three parents say texting is hurting their kid's performance in school. The good news is that today's teenagers are reading and writing more than ever; unfortunately, what they're reading and writing are barely literate texts from fellow barely literate friends, such as: C U L8R, not :(.

The result? Only half of Americans between ages 18 and 24 have read a book other than ones required at school or work, the lowest reading level of any adult group younger than age 75.

"Texting Makes U Stupid," blares the title of a *Newsweek* article. As proof, they cite an alarming statistic: The gap in reading ability between

15-year-olds in Shanghai and those in the U.S. is now as big as the gap between the U.S. and rural regions in Chile. Scary.

Yet, if a parent needs to reach a child in a pinch, texting is the fastest, easiest, least intrusive way. Texting is a classic double-edged sword. What's a parent to do?

Unplugged Parenting

One parent, Susan Maushart, did what millions of tuned-out parents have threatened to do—she unplugged her three teenagers. For six months, she took away the Internet, the TV, iPods, iPads, cellphones, and video games. She wrote about the experiment in her book, *The Winter of Our Disconnect*. The result: She and her kids rediscovered the small pleasures in life—playing board games, reading books, listening to music as a family instead of four heads bobbing to their own iTune favorites.

Maushart decided to unplug the family because her three teenagers "didn't just use media, they inhabited media," she wrote. The biggest danger of the social grid, as she saw it, was that her girls "had become mere accessories of their own social networking profile, as if real life were simply a dress rehearsal (or more accurately, a photo op) for the next status update."

In all fairness, teenagers aren't the only ones hooked on the digital grid—after a slow start, their parents are catching up. As I'm writing this sentence, I hear the "bing" that an email just arrived. No hesitation—I click on it. I'm back in five seconds. It was spam.

Today, in the age of the always-on Internet, parents, and even grandparents, are guilty of not just "using media," as we do when we read the newspaper, but, of "inhabiting media," as Maushart observes in her kids. For example, I have two dear friends, a married couple, she in her 50s, he well into his 60s, who spend half their time staring into their laps at their smartphones during our occasional dinners out.

They participate in our conversations, as always, but they become super-energized when someone makes an innocuous comment, such as, "I wonder how old Abraham Lincoln was when he was assassinated." The comment zaps them like a tazer; they suddenly spring to life, eyes and

92

hands all over their iPhones, snapping at the question like a hungry hyena at a Honeybaked Ham.

Oh, Lincoln was 56 at the time of his death. Thanks, Google....

Information Overload

Truth is, in the flood of trivial information, we're all drowning. Each day the average American spends 12 hours consuming information, taking in more than 100,000 words and thousands more visuals in the form of pictures, photos, and graphics.

The digital grid is gobbling up our lives, one click at a time.

A case in point: Let's say you spend a total of two hours each day posting on Facebook or Twitter and surfing the Web in ways that do not measurably improve your productivity at work or home. During the course of a year, that two hours a day adds up to about 30 days of wasted time. That's nearly 10% of your year—poof, dissolved into cyberspace. And what have you got to show for it? You learned Justin Bieber wrecked his Lamborghini....

Big whoop.

Far and away the most popular app for smartphones is Angry Birds, a digital game in which players slingshot cartoon birds at their egg-stealing pig foes. To date, 50 million Angry Bird apps have been downloaded.

Everyone who needs to go on a "digital diet," raise your hand.

The Helpful Edge of Tech

To be fair, Angry Birds is just one of 500,000 apps available for downloading at the Apple App Store. "There's an app for that," says the iPhone advertisement. And many of those apps can help you live a life of independence by saving you time and money and making you more productive in all areas of your life.

For sure people can waste vast amounts of time playing silly games on their smartphones and posting on Facebook. But Facebook, like the Internet, can inform and educate as well as entertain. It can even be used as a tool to liberate millions of people, as happened in the Arab Spring.

93

First, some Facebook facts: As I write this, one out of every dozen people on this planet has a Facebook account. In just seven years, Facebook has wired together a twelfth of humanity into a single network. Nearly 50% of Americans have a Facebook account, but 70% of users live outside the U.S. If Facebook were a country, it would be the third-largest behind China and India.

That can add up to billions of wasted minutes each month as millions of users upload goofy photos and post snarky comments on friends' sites. The opportunity to waste vast amounts of time—that's the downside of social media and the Internet. The upside? Independence. And not just for individuals, but for entire nations.

It Takes Social Media 20 Days to Unseat 30 Years

In late January of 2011, Egyptians took to the streets to protest the autocratic and corrupt government of President Mubarak, who had ruled the country for 30 years. A bunch of young people using social media, mainly Facebook and Twitter, were able to mobilize not just a few people... or even a few thousand people... but 50,000 people in a matter of days. At the height of the protests, millions of Egyptians marched to protest police brutality, government corruption, and high unemployment.

The revolution was led not by a religious figure or politician or military officer, as typically happened in past revolutions, but by 30-year-old Google executive, Wael Ghonim. Ghonim created a Facebook page called "We Are All Khaled Said," named after a young Egyptian businessman who died after being brutally beaten by Mubarak's state-sponsored police. The Facebook page attracted 500,000 members and became a rallying point against government abuses.

Facebook accounts were then used to plan, organize, and publicize protests. Social media took the place of the state-run newspapers and TV stations, which Egyptians hadn't trusted for decades.

"This is an Internet revolution," Ghonim said. "I'll call it Revolution 2.0." Facebook helped organize people, while Twitter was used to amplify

94

the situation, enabling protestors to share news and comment in real time as events unfolded. Less than 20 days after the first protests, Mubarak resigned, ending his 30-year seemingly immutable stranglehold on power.

Slash!—30 years of absolute power cut down in only 20 days. That's the helpful edge of the tech sword slashing its path to independence.

Networking Taken to New Levels

How do you comb through 500,000 apps to find the ones that can increase your independence? By asking others to recommend apps for scheduling... apps for quick, healthy meals... apps for at-home exercises... apps, in short, that will foster independence by saving time and money.

There are even apps that help you expand your circle of valuable friends and acquaintances. An iPhone app called Highlight and its Android equivalent, Glancee, track your location and notify you when friends—or even strangers you may want to meet—are nearby.

Based on what is called a "so-mo" (social-mobile) platform, these apps combine GPS location data with information you and people sitting nearby have published about yourselves on your Facebook profiles. The app notifies you when your profile and the profile of someone nearby show commonalities, such as growing up in the same city or majoring in the same subject in college. The developers envision a time when everyone has a so-mo app in their pockets, sending and receiving information to like-minded people like a radar beacon.

"The purpose of Highlight is to give you a sixth sense of the world around you and to surface the hidden connections that have always existed but that we've never before been able to see, " says co-founder and CEO Paul Davison.

"The way we discover new people is and always has been incredibly inefficient," continues Davison. "If we could just improve this process, we'd make this world such a better place." And potentially a friendlier, more connected place. If you're sitting at an outside café for lunch, Highlight will tell you that a co-worker is inside or that the person sitting one table over attended the same college as your sister.

Amazing stuff, isn't it? It's as if you could read someone's mind, and they could read yours. And to think this technology is just getting started.

Activity Versus Productivity

A former business partner of mine had a great expression and used it often. Two or three times a week he'd blurt, "Never confuse activity with productivity." A lot of wisdom packed into those five words.

But in the age of email, video mail, You Tube, Facebook, blogging, Twitter, and half a million apps, it's easy to confuse activity with productivity. If someone tweets 100 times a day, they could be wasting an hour in a useless *activity*… or they could be using the medium productively by motivating their team and furthering everyone's goals.

Years ago the great American naturalist and philosopher Henry David Thoreau observed that when a man buys a horse-drawn carriage, he doesn't own the carriage, the carriage owns him. Why? Because he has to spend time and money feeding and grooming the horses, cleaning the wagon, greasing the axles, repairing the spokes on the wood wheels… all of which takes more of his time and more of his money. He becomes, in a sense, a slave to the needs of the carriage, so the carriage owns him.

Likewise, social media will own you if the time and money you spend Tweeting and gaming and surfing and posting just drifts into cyberspace with nothing to show for it, which is, sadly to say, what happens to most people who are wired to the max.

For a growing part of the population, tech isn't a tool, it's a tyrant.

So, before you download another app or post another photo on your Facebook page, ask yourself these questions:

Do I own this medium?... Or does it own me?

Am I being merely active?... Or truly productive?

Is tech my tool?… Or my tyrant?

And finally, and most importantly—am I becoming addicted to the excitement and glow of technology?… Or is technology helping me live—and love—a life of independence?

You Can't Have Independence without Interdependence
(Work with People, Not for People)

How to Make Every Day Independence Day

You Can't Have Independence without Interdependence
(Work <u>with</u> People, Not <u>for</u> People)

If you want happiness for an hour, take a nap.
If you want happiness for a year, inherit a fortune.
If you want happiness for a lifetime, help others.

—Chinese proverb

Here are two short quizzes emailed to me by a life-long friend. See how many you can answer correctly:

Quiz 1: Rich and Famous people

1. Name the five wealthiest people in the world.
2. Name the last five Heisman Trophy winners.
3. Name the last five winners of the Miss Universe pageant.
4. Name the last five male Academy Award winners.
5. Name the head coaches of the last five Super Bowl winners.

How did you do? I'd be shocked if you got five of the 25 answers correct. Now try quiz 2:

Quiz 2: People Who Have Shaped You

1. List five teachers or mentors who made a difference in your life.
2. List five people who helped you through a tough time.
3. Name five people who taught you a useful skill or strategy.
4. Name five people who made you feel special or appreciated.
5. List five people you enjoy spending time with.

Much easier to answer the questions in the second quiz, isn't it?

The lesson?

The people who make a difference in your life are not the richest in the world. Or prettiest. Or the most famous. The people who mean the most to *you* are simply the ones you feel connected to... the people who have touched you in a meaningful way... who care about you... who you can trust.

Conservative columnist David Brooks, author of the best-seller *The Social Animal*, says we humans are caught up in the "loneliness loop," the universal yearning to feel part of a community, to feel we belong, to feel accepted and understood by others in our group.

In short, just as humans have an inborn need for *independence*, they also have an inborn need for *interdependence*. Which means, ironically, that to become independent, we must first be dependent on acceptance by others within a community, whether it's a cause, a religion, a club, a team, a business, a family—or all the above.

Love: Modern Proof of an Ancient Miracle Cure

Solitary confinement is a special form of punishment that isolates individuals from human contact. Although people locked in solitary are alone, they're anything but independent. In fact, other than infants, people locked in solitary are the most dependent people in the world because they have to rely on their captors for all their basic needs, such as food, water, and diversion from sensory deprivation and the suffocating sameness, oftentimes weeks and months at a stretch.

Opponents consider solitary confinement a form of torture because lack of human contact for as little as a week can lead to depression and psychoses, seeding mental and physical illnesses in otherwise healthy people.

In short, humans are, indeed, "social animals," and our ability to form long-term, meaningful bonds with fellow humans sets us apart from the rest of the animal kingdom (although recent research has shown that some animals, like unrelated same-sex chimpanzees, baboons, and dolphins, can develop strong bonds, similar to our friendships, that can last for years).

If social isolation is harmful to humans, is the converse true—the richer our relationships, the healthier we are? Absolutely. Recent research proves what poets and prophets have been saying for thousands of years—the best cure for what ails the body, as well as the soul, is love and friendship.

"Love can actually make us healthier," says health expert Lisa Collier Cool. "Love can lengthen your life, ward off stress, boost your immune system, lower your blood pressure, protect you from colds and flu, blunt your response to pain, hasten wound healing, and lower your risk of dementia in old age."

Improved Relationships Lead to Independence

Because we can't have independence without interdependence, doesn't it make sense to expand and improve the relationships in our lives? Of course. In the coming pages, you will learn the *Top 10 Tips* for improving all your relationships—with co-workers... children... spouses... even best buddies you have known for years.

Relationships are like flowers—your job isn't done when you plant them... your job is just starting. To grow, relationships need constant weeding, watering, and fertilizing. Yes, nurturing plants and people takes time and patience, but in the end, like flowers, well-tended relationships grow and bloom, and they are beautiful.

Top 10 Tips for Improving Relationships

Tip 1: Ask Questions Instead of Making Statements: No one likes being told what to do, especially if the order-giver is a peer or has an equal amount of power in the relationship. Everybody, on the other hand, likes to act in their own best interest and likes being part of a team, to participate willingly instead of being forced to follow orders. The best way to do that is to couch your opinions and phrase your "orders" as questions. That way people can feel like they own their response. A good friend of mine used this technique to defuse a potentially explosive conversation with his wife. The wife was a teacher earning about $60,000 a year who wanted to retire 10 years before her full retirement age. Rather than tell her they couldn't afford it, my friend handled the situation by calmly asking a question: "Fine, dear. If that's what you want. But by retiring early, you will earn $20,000 less per year than if you waited until full retirement age. So, while I locate our monthly budget, I want you to think about this: 'Where can you and I cut $1,700 a month to accommodate our reduced household income?'" After glancing at the family budget, she quickly decided that early retirement wasn't a good idea after all.

Tip 2: Give Five Positive Statements for Each Negative One: Studies show that the brain has a "negativity bias," meaning negatives have a much greater impact on our brain than positives. The negativity bias is why personal insults or criticism hit us harder and stay with us longer. It's why negative ads in political campaigns are more effective than positive ones. It's also why one positive comment or action cannot offset one negative one. If you say, "You forgot to take out the trash *again*"... and then 15 minutes later say, "Thanks for giving the kids a bath," you're not back to even because the negative far outweighs the positive. How many positives does it take to keep a relationship healthy? Marriage expert Dr. John Gottman says the formula should be five positives to one negative for married couples. Any ratio less than 5:1 predicts unhappiness and potentially divorce.

Tip 3: Make "Yes, and…" Statements Build Consensus: An improv comedy group calling themselves Four-Day Weekend conduct corporate workshops to teach employees how to improve creativity and foster teamwork by using the "yes, and…" principle: One performer feeds a line so another performer can be funny, such as: "We should go to the lake this weekend"; the other performer expands on the line by saying, *"Yes, and…"* followed by something like, *"…* we should take our pets with us"; this line opens the door for the next performer to add a ridiculous twist to the narrative by adding their own, "Yes, and…" statement. The technique works great for brainstorming sessions at work or with the family: Dad might start with, "We should go on a cruise," and then encourage Mom and the kids to elaborate with their own "Yes, and…" statements. Silly as it sounds, it works.

Tip 4: Make "I" Statements Instead of "You" Statements: This is a staple strategy taught by marriage counselors and therapists everywhere. When a husband or wife makes a negative comment to their spouse in the form of a "you statement," such as, "You never discipline the kids," the speaker comes off as superior, which will only make the target of the criticism defensive, intensifying the conflict. Instead, if the spouse phrases the comment as an "I statement," such as "I feel I'm the one who has to discipline the kids most of the time," the speaker sounds like an equal in the relationship. That small rhetorical shift changes the statement from a bold criticism to a more neutral statement that can be discussed more rationally.

Tip 5: Understand the Difference between Arguing and Persuading: Attorneys argue. Salespeople persuade. They both have the same goal— to prevail at the end of the discussion. But they use totally different approaches to "winning." If you're a prosecutor *arguing* your side of the case to a judge and jury, you want to *win* the argument by blowing holes in the defense and pinning the defendant to the wall. You don't care if the defendant's feelings are hurt—your goal is to win, period. But when you're in a discussion with your child or spouse, there's no third-party judge and jury—*they* are the judge and jury. So, *you do care about their feelings* because you have to face them the next day. And the next. With friends and family, frame your discussions in terms of *persuasion*, which means building bridges based on empathy and common goals to help guide them to your side of the issue. A wise attorney understands that if he wants a good relationship with his wife and children, he will restrict his arguments to the courtroom, not the family living room.

Tip 6: Praise in Public; Punish in Private: I first learned this rule when I was teaching high school back in the 1970s and '80s, and it was reinforced when I was raising my daughter, Sydney. Think back to the times you were scolded by a parent in front of your friends…. Made you feel embarrassed, even ashamed, didn't it? And angry, too, I bet. But if you dared direct your anger at your parent with your friends around, then the scene got even uglier. Hey, kids need reprimanding from time to time—that's a big part of parenting. But if it's done in private, the message still gets delivered and the child (or student or subordinate at work) won't have to deal with the double-dose of pain. Likewise, when you praise people in public, you're edifying them in front of their peers, which raises a person's status in the group. Remember how you felt when you marched up to receive a badge or trophy at an awards ceremony? Made you feel proud, didn't it? So does praise in public.

Tip 7: Shape Your Message So That the Listener Can Hear It: I've played sports all my life, and I coached high school tennis for 10-plus years. I learned that the best coaches script their messages differently for different players. Some players respond well and perform better when a coach gets in their face and screams. Other players will freeze up when screamed at; others get angry and scream back. The coach could be delivering the same message in the same way to three different players and get two negative reactions and only one positive one, a success rate of only 33%. That's why good coaches and good parents and good managers shape their messages for their audience. You can deliver the most profound, helpful message in the world, but if the audience shuts you out, what good does it do you or the audience? None—and it may even do damage to your relationship. If you want the audience to respond to your message, anticipate how your message will be received and then pick the time… the tone… the place… and the medium (email? text? face-to-face?...) that will increase the likelihood that the message will be received and acted upon.

Tip 8: When Delivering Bad News, Blame the Board: It's natural for people to confuse the message with the messenger, especially when the messenger is delivering bad news. We've all witnessed a furious airline passenger berate a flight attendant for asking the passenger to put their carry-on luggage in the overhead bin instead of letting it sit in the empty seat next to the passenger. A simple way to defuse an escalating argument is to "blame the board." Calmly explain that it's not *your* rule you're enforcing; you're only doing what the board of directors (or FAA or school board or county ordinance) tells you to do. Sometimes it helps to explain the reasoning behind the rule (the luggage could become a flying missile during turbulence); sometimes it helps to agree with the person that the rule is silly or outdated or whatever, but that your job is to enforce the rule or you could be the one in big trouble. Be calm. Be polite. Be sympathetic, even. But keep blaming the board until the conversation is over.

Tip 9: Your First Move Is to Help: The best way to strengthen a relationship is to do something for another person. Humans always act in their own best interest, and if you help them further their interest, they'll appreciate the gesture and feel obliged to help you out some day. A study of professional negotiators showed that the most successful negotiators searched for shared interests by asking questions and then offering ways to help the other side get what they wanted without giving away the store. One of the first things to say to a new acquaintance or to a friend who is struggling with an issue is, "How can I help?" When you help a person, you move the relationship from a loose connection to a deeper bond. "You cooperate and sacrifice because you want to help a friend in need," says Reid Hoffman, founder of the social media site, LinkedIn (with 130 million users and growing) and author of *The Start-up of You*. "But you also help others because you figure you'll be able to call on them in the future when you are the one in the bind. That isn't being selfish. It's being human."

Tip 10: Lots of Little Things Mean More Than One Big Thing: A recent scientific study confirmed what women have known for centuries: "Small positive marital acts frequently performed affect marriage quality more strongly than large gestures irregularly enacted." Freshening your spouse's coffee or buttering her bagel without being asked... pitching in with the laundry... walking the dog (even though that's not your job) on a nasty winter morning when he's in a rush to get to a meeting—these and dozens of small, generous gestures are what counselors say is the key to happy marriages. These small gestures make a big statement—"I care about you." Small kindnesses are easy to do. But easy *not* to do. And that's why they carry so much weight.

Men, especially, figure the big gesture—the anniversary cruise or gold Rolex on her birthday—will make up for neglecting the daily gestures of thoughtfulness. Sorry, fellas... it doesn't work that way.

Small kindnesses say "I love you" more than spoken words ever can. "Your actions speak so loud I can't hear what you're saying," goes the old expression. Words of wisdom we all need to heed in our over-booked, budget-strapped, pressure-packed world.

People. It's been said that we can't live with 'em... and we can't live without 'em. But then, who would want to?

Since we can't live without 'em, we might as well nurture the relationships that mean the most to us. In the end, the richest people in the world are the ones with the richest relationships.

CONCLUSION

Trust Your Hip!

CONCLUSION

Trust Your Hip!

Never let the fear of striking out get in your way.
—Babe Ruth

October 19, 2011, is a date I won't forget—with each painless step I take, I'm reminded that October 19 was the day I underwent surgery to replace my right hip.

At 11:00 a.m. I was being wheeled into the operating room.

At 4:30 p.m. a nurse was walking me around the hospital corridor.

The miracle of modern medicine.

"Did the hip surgery hurt?" people ask. "I don't know," I reply. "I was asleep." But I do know that for two years leading up to the surgery, my hip hurt a little… then a lot… then so much I couldn't cross my leg to tie my shoe… couldn't lift my leg high enough to get on my bike… couldn't sleep on my right side… couldn't walk from one end of the house to the other without grabbing onto a chair back or countertop for support.

I could have tolerated the pain a few more months… a few more years, perhaps. But not the incapacitation. Not the humiliation of having to add a child's booster seat to my dining room chair so I could bend less when I sat down to eat.

My hip had gotten so stiff and painful I had to choose between surgery and a wheelchair.

I chose surgery.

Here I am, six months later, swimming and running and biking pain free. Was I scared to have the surgery? Sure was. Lots of things can go wrong in a three-hour operation. But by October the *reward* of being pain free and independent outweighed the *risk* of a botched operation or a nasty infection.

Post-Op Therapy Is the Toughest Part

There are more than 1 million hip and knee replacements in the U.S. each year, and as Baby Boomers age and technology improves, that number will go up.

The toughest part of having a joint replaced isn't the pain. Pain meds take care of that. Stiffness and swelling were the hardest things to accommodate, especially in the first couple weeks. With my right leg swollen down to my black-and-blue toes, it was awkward getting in and out of bed. Awkward sleeping on my back. Awkward getting dressed. Awkward getting in and out of a chair.

And using a walker and later a cane in my left hand took some getting used to—again, awkward.

The hardest part of recovering from orthopedic surgery is the rehabilitation therapy, rehab for short. Here's what you can expect: The first two weeks a therapist visits you at home three days a week, helping you strengthen and loosen your hip with leg lifts and side-to-side movements that are insanely simple if you have a good hip, but gruntingly hard if you've just had your leg sawed on a few days before. By the end of the second week, you'll graduate to out-patient therapy, a facility typically located in a strip mall and staffed by a half-dozen licensed physical therapists.

I was assigned to Kendall, a smart, smiling brunette from Chicago who had earned a doctorate in physical therapy. I was in good hands—kind, caring, compassionate hands—or so I thought. Turns out she was one part Mother Teresa, two parts Vince Lombardi.

No Pain, No Gain

Three times a week, for an hour at a time, Kendall would alternately cajole me with soothing words of encouragement ("That's it... You can do it... Just three more squats") and bark at me to fight through the stiffness and, yes, pain ("Come on, man up!... Act like you've been here before... What are you doing using your arms, that's cheating. Start over!")

Three times a week for six weeks Kendall cooed and scolded me through drills that had me squatting to pick up plastic cups... stepping over and around small traffic cones... shuffling sideways across the room with giant rubber bands looped around my ankles.

They kept the room temperature fixed at 72 degrees.

I sweated like I was in a sauna.

But at the end of six weeks, I was released. Or should I say expelled—the insurance covering the out-patient therapy had reached its limit. On the way out the door, Kendall gave me a hug and a tee shirt and told me I had been a great patient.

I cherish the hug and kind words. And I still have the tee shirt.

I'm not going to lie—physical therapy is frustrating. More frustrating than painful, actually. Things that you take for granted before arthritis sets in, such as squatting down to pick a sock off the carpet... or raising your leg high enough to step over a threshold... these are tough to do a few weeks after surgery.

I was surprised that pain wasn't the biggest challenge in rehab—I was prepared to deal with that. What I wasn't prepared for was a mental challenge—fear.

Fear that I'd fall.

Fear that I'd tear the incision (my 5-inch incision was glued instead of sutured, making me even more fearful it would pull apart).

Fear that I'd bend too far or squat too deep and tear a muscle or dislocate my hip.

The physical therapists reassured me time and again that dislocations are rare. And that muscle tears were rarer still. But constant reassurance didn't matter to me—I was still overly cautious... still holding back.

Trust Your Hip

I remember the moment I got past my fear. I was in the second week with Kendall, still fearful, going through the motions during an exercise but not committing myself to a full range of motion.

Kendall looked up from her laptop where she logged her students' progress, furrowed her brow, and barked, *Trust your hip*!

"What?" I said defensively.

"Trust your hip," she said. "It's stronger than you think. You're in more danger of hurting your recovery than hurting your hip. It's been a month since your surgery. The muscles have healed by now. New bone is growing around your implant. There's no way you're going to hurt yourself doing these exercises. Trust your hip."

And I did.

I started squatting lower on my knee bends. Stretching wider on my sideways shuffles. Crossing my right ankle over my left knee faster. Walking without a limp. Trusting my hip and getting stronger by the day.

Today, six months after my surgery, I trust my surgically repaired right hip more than my "good" left hip, which, I cringe to think about, is starting to ache a bit after my daily walk or bike ride.

My History of 'Trusting My Hip'

I'm telling you this story to remind you that we all have times in our lives when we need to "trust our hips" by letting go and trusting ourselves.

When I left for college at 18, I had my doubts about my abilities as a student. But I trusted that I was at least as smart as the average freshman. And I was right. Today I have three degrees. And I'm planning to take more classes at the local university.

When I bought my first house in 1974 for $15,000, it was the worst house in a good neighborhood... a real "handyman special," in realtors' language. At the time I'd never done any renovation other than painting my bedroom at home. So I had to trust that I could buy the right tools and make the right repairs to turn a decrepit little house into a charming little cottage. It took me two years (and more than a few miscues that I had to do over), but I sold that house for twice what I paid for it and used the profits to buy a $50,000 house in a great neighborhood—and my 40-year career investing in real estate was born.

When I resigned from teaching in 1986, I had no job lined up... no contacts in Tampa, where I was determined to live. And no experience in running my own business. But I trusted I could meet people and learn what I needed to know to open and operate a successful business. I figured what I couldn't do myself I would hire others to do. And that's what I did. More than 25 years later, I own two profitable businesses, publishing and real estate investing.

My two business endeavors have allowed me to be self-employed and independent going into my fourth decade.

And it all started with trusting I could perform outside my comfort zone... trusting my hip, so to speak.

What Hip Do You Have to Trust?

This is a book about independence. But it's not about how I became independent. It's about how *you* can become independent in an increasingly job-dependent, government-dependent world.

Independence starts with *thinking* you WANT to be independent... *thinking* you NEED to be independent... then *believing* you CAN be independent.

Trusting yourself, in other words.

Look, other people have trusted you in the past, isn't that true? When an employer hired you, they trusted you could do the job you were assigned, right? When your spouse married you, they trusted you would make a great companion to go through life with. When a college or trade school admitted you, they trusted you had the smarts and ambition to pass the courses and graduate with a degree, correct?

Think of all the times other people have trusted you in the past—with jobs. With responsibilities. With assignments. Well, don't you think it's time to trust yourself?

Look, I know independence sounds scary, especially if all you've ever done is work for someone else. But I bet some of the businesses you worked for in the past were successful. And those businesses were owned by someone who started out as an employee... someone who was dependent on a job, just like you. But someone who had a dream to own their own life by owning their own business.

If they can do it, you can do it, too.

So, trust your hip. Trust your ability to learn... and grow... and lead... and persevere... and rebound from your setbacks and leap forward from your successes.

Trust your hip.

Your hip—your talents, your dream—is stronger than you think. But you'll never know until you test it... put some pressure on it... trust it!

Once you do that, you'll be stronger. And happier. And eventually, seemingly magically, you'll be living—and loving—a life of independence!